Man of the Millennium

The Age of Joseph of Nazareth

SEQUEL

The Once and Future Family

Jesus, Mary and Joseph

R.A. Varghese

TESTAMENT Book House

228 Park Ave S
PMB 19611
New York, New York 10003-1502

ISBN 978-1-7364447-2-6

Copyright © 2021 by R.A. Varghese

All rights reserved. No part of this publication may be reproduced, stored in a retrieval system, or transmitted, in any form or by any means, electronic, mechanical, photocopying, recording, or otherwise, without the prior permission of Roy Abraham Varghese.

Published May 2021

R.A. Varghese is the author and/or editor of sixteen books on the interface of science, philosophy, and religion. His *Cosmos, Bios, Theos*, included contributions from 24 Nobel Prize-winning scientists. *Time* magazine called *Cosmos* "the year's most intriguing book about God." *Cosmic Beginnings and Human Ends*, a subsequent work, won a Templeton Book Prize for "*Outstanding Books in Science and Natural Theology.*" His *The Wonder of the World* was endorsed by leading thinkers include two Nobelists and was the subject of an Associated Press story. He co-authored *There is a God—How the World's Most Notorious Atheist Changed His Mind* with Antony Flew (a book translated into Spanish, Portuguese, Korean, Russian, and Arabic). His most recent work, *The Missing Link* (2013), includes contributions from three Nobel Prize winners and scientists from Oxford, Cambridge, Harvard, and Yale. Varghese was a panelist at the science and religion forum in the Parliament of World Religions held in Chicago in 1993 and an invitee and participant in the Millennium World Peace Summit of Religious and Spiritual Leaders held at the United Nations in August 2000. Varghese has been interviewed on numerous radio and TV shows including *Coast to Coast*. He has also been profiled in different print publications.

Man of the Millennium
The Age of Joseph of Nazareth

Contents

In the Fullness of Time 1

The Seven Signs....................................... 15
   *Heaven has spoken – Encounters
      of the Third Order* 37
   Dreamer and Doer – the Biblical Story 57
   The Testimony of "Tradition" 122
   The Saints' Saint 132
   Theological Momentum 142
   Devotional Crescendo 158
   The Church says "Yes" 174

Application 195

In the Fullness of Time

The Greatest "Sighting" of the Millennium

This book is about the most dramatic theological "sighting" of the millennium. In our present day, Heaven has drawn us to the recognition of Joseph, the virginal father of Jesus and chaste husband of Mary. Here we will briefly review the "equations" and "experiments," the "signs and wonders," that led to our "finding" the Father of Jesus.

The Bible tells us that God reveals himself, his plans and purposes, only after human hearts and minds have been suitably prepared and primed: "But when the fullness of time had come, God sent his Son, born of a woman, born under the law, to ransom those under the law, so that we might receive adoption." (*Galatians* 4:4-5). This is true not simply of the primordial revelation chronicled in the books of the Bible but equally of the progressive understanding and assimilation of the mysteries revealed to us in the incarnation of God in Jesus

Christ. Each advancement in our comprehension presupposes the grasp of previous insights.

For instance, the dogmatic definition of the Blessed Virgin Mary as Mother of God in 431 AD (Ephesus) presupposed the dogmatic definition of Jesus Christ as God and Man in 325 AD (Nicea).

Moreover, new divinely guided insights historically have (not coincidentally) been especially effective in addressing problems specific to the time in which they were articulated. A deeper insight into St. Joseph and his Holy Family is especially applicable in our post-family era.

Just as the Christian world recognized Jesus' identity in all its fullness in the first millennium and that of Mary his mother in the second millennium, we are now positioned to understand the Joseph we never knew in this third Christian millennium.[1] In retrospect, it seems obvious that a true appreciation for St. Joseph could come only after a fuller understanding of Jesus and Mary. Once we had come to see that Jesus was indeed the Divine Logos incarnate and that Mary was the Mother of the Logos in his human nature, it was natural to inquire further into the man linked to one as father and to the other as husband.

The recognition of Joseph is vital on both a strategic and a tactical level. Strategically, it is part of our continuing understanding of the full magnitude of the revelation of God in Christ and God as Trinity. We can fully understand the Gospel Jesus only if we grasp the formative role played not just by his mother but also his father ("He went down with them and came to Nazareth, and was obedient to them." *Luke* 2:51).

At a tactical level, given the obstacles to salvation and sanctification in our life on earth, we need all the help we can get. St. Joseph whom God appointed the guardian of the Holy Family is also the God-given guardian of the human family. But it is a guardianship that can only be bestowed upon request – whether it be from individuals, the Church or the world.

Findings Scientific and Theological

But first a word about our talk of this as a "finding."

We talk of findings in the world of divine revelation because, as with the great findings of science, there are findings too in understanding what has been revealed – the findings of theology. In both science and theology, such findings presuppose and leverage the breakthroughs of the past. Sometimes they change all our perspectives helping us see the older findings in a new light (Einsteinian physics subsumes the physics of Newton). Scientific findings, of course, concern what is physically measurable while theology relates to realities that transcend the sensory. Nevertheless, they both advance our knowledge of the Real World. And to this extent the breakthroughs of an Augustine and an Aquinas are just as significant as the triumphs of a Newton or an Einstein. Theological truths, in fact, are immeasurably more important for the human person than scientific theories because these truths concern the meaning and purpose of life and our eternal destiny.

The recognition of Joseph led to yet another major affiliated finding, much as the Theory of Relativity began with Special Relativity and culminated in General Relativity. The recognition of Joseph of Nazareth came to a climax with the finding of the immediate family of God-become-man as a reality in its own right. The finding of the Holy Family of Nazareth could only come after the finding that it *was a family*. And this required the recovery of the biblical revelation that Joseph was the true husband of Mary and the true yet virginal father of Jesus. This was, of course, a process of theological and not scientific understanding. But the two-fold finding was and is dramatic because of its inevitable impact on human society, human history and our very understanding of God.

So why Joseph and the Holy Family and why now? And why should it matter?

As it happens, this discovery is the latest event in the prophetic roadmap that is Christian history. By "prophetic" we mean something different from the future tense.

Of course, since the beginning of the Christian dispensation, a few of the faithful have turned their gaze to the end of time. Often their theology and day-to-day priorities have been shaped by their views of the Second Coming of Jesus Christ and attendant events. In fact, recent decades have seen a proliferation of competing "end-time" timeframes, scenarios and deadlines – all of which are regularly revised.

But "prophecy," as we use it here, concerns God's action *in the present* as it pertains to our salvation, sanctification and schooling in the sacred mysteries. Prophecy in this sense, scholars have said, is not fore-telling but forth-telling: proclaiming the Mind of God. The future in itself is less our concern than the present precisely because God wants us to focus on the here-and-now: "'In an acceptable time I heard you, and on the day of salvation I helped you.'

Behold, now is a very acceptable time; behold, now is the day of salvation." (2 *Corinthians* 6:2).

We are not asked to make guesses about the future but to prayerfully discern and cooperate with the present-day workings of Providence. And it is here that we apprehend, first, the prophetic role of Joseph of Nazareth, *the* man of the third Christian millennium, and, climactically, of his Holy Family, the representative on earth of the Holy Trinity.

An Overview of the Great Theological Discoveries

But how do we discover truths within revelation, the truths of theology? Let us note first that, at any given time, the process of deciphering the supernal code, of recognizing the divine design embedded in everyday events – the prophetic dimension of history – is neither instantaneous nor complete. There is an obvious sequence to the way in which the Plan of Providence is unveiled and understood much as there is a sequence to the movement in cosmic and biological history that culminates in Homo sapiens.

Even a cursory review of salvation history makes this clear. The mind of Israel had to first be weaned away from superstition and brought to the one true God, then the Messiah had to be born so as to bring about the redemption of humanity and finally his Apostles had to proclaim his Gospel to all peoples.

The proclamation of the Good News was three-fold: living the commandments of Christ by administering the sacraments; creating and disseminating definitive records of the life and message of the Savior; and, finally, formulating an organic body of doctrine that authoritatively crystallized the Christian revelation.

From the writing of the Gospels to the preaching of the salvific message, from the dispensing of the sacraments to the definition of dogma, the initiative, impetus and governance came from God but the execution was dependent on the cooperation of humanity – albeit that portion of humanity receptive to the divine message and responsive to the promptings of the Spirit.

The revelation of God and the discernment of its meaning, then, inevitably had to be tailored to human limitation. The Messiah himself spent his first thirty years in obscurity. And even in the three years he proclaimed the Kingdom, he revealed his true identity only toward the end ("And he asked them, 'But who do you say that I am?' Peter said to him in reply, 'You are the Messiah.' Then he warned them not to tell anyone about him." *Mark* 8:29-30).

Subsequent Christian history followed the same staging pattern resulting in a chronological sequence running into centuries in which one divinely guided insight followed another and then another on an ongoing basis. It was only in the fifth century that the canon of the New Testament was fixed. The first Christological dogma was defined only in the fourth century and the first Marian dogma in the fifth. Further Christological and Trinitarian clarifications and definitions continued in Council after Council to the seventh century.

At the foundation of the story of salvation lies the Triune God and the divine Incarnation. One might say that the first Christian millennium was the era of understanding and articulating this fundamental revelation while correcting deviations and distortions.

But once it absorbed the reality of the Son of God-made-man and the Holy Trinity, the Christian mind was drawn by the next horizon of discovery, the Mother of God.

Thus, in the next millennium, the first and second century proclamation of the Blessed Virgin as New Eve blossomed into a body of theological truth nurtured by the saints, mystics, Doctors and Popes of the Church. The ancient Fathers of the Church,

East and West, and the earliest liturgies had already created a corpus of Marian insight. Now St. Bernard of Clairvaux, St. Dominic, St. Thomas Aquinas, John Duns Scotus, St. Louis Marie de Montfort, St. Maximilian Kolbe and others mined these rich veins to yield a treasure trove for the faithful. And the unpacking of the New Eve revelation that began with the dogmatic Conciliar definitions of Mary as Mother of God (Ephesus), perpetual Virgin (Constantinople II) and intercessor (Nicaea II) reached a climax in the second millennium with the proclamation of her immaculate conception (Pius IX) and assumption into Heaven (Pius XII) and her being Mother of the Church (Vatican II).

The next frontier of discovery emerged well before the close of the second millennium. Just as the discovery of Mary had begun in the first millennium, the second millennium saw a new and sustained focus on the third member of the family of Jesus.

In 2020, Pope Francis declared 2020-2021 the Year of St. Joseph, an unprecedented recognition of St. Joseph's role in salvation history. In his declaration, the Pope also linked St. Joseph to the Heavenly Father – "In his relationship to Jesus, Joseph was the earthly shadow of the heavenly Father: he watched over him and protected him, never leaving him to go his own way."

Sts. Jerome, Ambrose and Augustine had already articulated the central theological truths about St. Joseph in the first half of the first millennium. But while devotion to St. Joseph had an early start in the East, it gained momentum in the West only at the turn of the first millennium. The first Western church bearing his name appeared in Bologna in 1129. Many of the great saints of the Middle Ages, St. Bernard, St. Thomas, St. Gertrude, St. Bridget of Sweden, were fervent devotees of the father of Jesus as were such later saints as St. Francis de Sales, St. Alphonsus Ligouri, St. Teresa of Avila, St. Bernadette of Lourdes and St. Teresa of Lisieux.

The Church's response came with Pope Pius IX's proclamation of Joseph as Patron of the Church and the unprecedented encyclicals of Popes Leo XIII and John Paul II in 1889 and 1989. Pope Pius X approved the Litany of St. Joseph and Pope John XXIII, in an extraordinary move, included St. Joseph in the canon of the Mass at the start of the Second Vatican Council (and the Council itself he placed under the protection of St. Joseph).

The finding of Joseph was momentous in its own right but, as we have said, it was a stepping-stone to a greater discovery yet. It was a prophetic milestone that unveiled a vision of human history and the human family immediately relevant to our daily lives. For the pilgrimage to Joseph does not stop with him. It takes us to his family. And once we consider the nature and role of this family, we discover new dimensions of it that became evident only over centuries. The insight into the Holy Family took place in parallel with the recognition of Joseph because almost all the Josephine saints, scholars and Popes had a great devotion to the Holy Family. As a result the Feast and Confraternity of the Holy Family received the enthusiastic support of the Church's Magisterium.

Why, it will be asked, was all this not visible from the very beginning? Are we simply inventing new "revelations" that detract from the all-sufficient and necessarily solitary majesty of the redemptive sacrifice of Christ? The answer is that everything about Joseph and his family was evident right at the start but we did not have eyes to see nor ears to hear. It took seven centuries just to comprehensively articulate the identity of Jesus. Is it any surprise that it would take many more centuries to ponder and probe the meaning of the family of Jesus, the Savior's immediate penumbra?

First Family

Moreover, the idea that there was no role for finite humans in the mission of Jesus simply contradicts the plain facts of the Gospel narratives such as the sending of the Apostles as well as New Testament texts like "Now I rejoice in my sufferings for your sake, and in my flesh I am filling up what is lacking in the afflictions of Christ on behalf of his body, which is the church." (*Colossians* 1:24)

All Christians agree that Jesus was the Word of God incarnate and that his sacrificial death redeemed humanity. But the truth of the Incarnation and the "effects" of the redemptive sacrifice had to be transmitted to all the world by free human agents.

Even more fundamental, we recognize now what is hidden in plain sight: the incarnation of God in Christ took place in and through a family: he was the virginal child of a married couple. The participation of the family went beyond the Incarnation and extended to the Son's redemptive mission: it was the father who was tasked with naming the Infant as "savior" and "birthing" him into the lineage of the Chosen People; it was the mother who was told she would be pierced with a sword as she participated in her Son's mission; and both parents were charged with protecting and nurturing their Child as they prepared him for his fateful mission. The redemption of humanity was achieved not as a solitary act but an act begotten in solidarity because it was an act into which the Redeemer drew his family.

The Holy Family, you might say, is the endgame on our earthly journey. Our awareness of the true significance of the Holy Family changes our whole perspective of human history and world events. For human history is salvation history and world events are Providentially-permitted events. And at the center of salvation history and the works of Providence we find Jesus Christ, God and Man, and *with him*, his immediate family, his earthly virgin father and virgin mother.

The father and the mother assisted the mission of the Son of God made man in a manner that was irreducibly distinct from the part played by his Apostles and other followers. They belonged to an "order" of action in salvation history that radically transcended the role played by all other human persons. As the Fathers of the Church recognized from the very beginning, Mary was the New Eve just as Jesus was the New Adam. Joseph, for his part, was both the "family tie" that bound the Savior of humanity to Adam, Abraham and David and the one chosen by God to protect and direct the New Adam and the New Eve. As obedient as the greatest patriarchs of Israel he was entrusted with a role and a responsibility that far surpassed anything entrusted to any human person: he was truly the husband of the Mother of God and truly albeit virginally the father of the Son of God.

There can be no home without a family and the Universe cannot be our home if we refuse to be part of the Family of its Creator. This is why the recognition of the Holy Family is not only timely but urgent.

The Seven Signs

It should be said that the discovery of Joseph has been made possible in the present day by a series of major breakthroughs. The saints and mystics had already pointed to his exalted position in the hierarchy of humanity. The greatest theologians of the Church laid the foundations for a biblically-grounded understanding of his role in salvation history and modern theologians have further explored the ramifications of the covenantal marriage of Joseph and Mary and his virginal fatherhood. Major modern apparitions "approved" as "worthy of belief" have featured St. Joseph. The Church herself brought the development of doctrine relating to Joseph to a climax and (among other things) officially proclaimed Joseph as her patron.

These happenings have not gone unnoticed and St. Joseph was even featured on the cover of *Time* magazine. Various Protestant writers have written books on the meaning of Joseph for the present day and his significance has been studied in Protestant publications like *Christianity Today*. One of the best-known Protestant theologians of the twentieth century, Karl Barth, known for his antagonism toward Mariology and Catholicism, was effusive in his praise for Joseph: "I love St. Joseph. I rejoiced when John XIII inserted his name in the Roman Canon. I intend to ask Paul VI to give him prominence. He protected the Child; he will protect the Church."[1] J.J. von Almen, a pastor of the Swiss Reformed Church, held that St. Joseph "was the guarantor before Israel of the messianic tradition and he is the model of male sanctity as is Our Lady of female holiness."[2] If there was ever a time that could be called the Age of Joseph, it would be today.

He existed

The first thing we have to realize about Joseph of Nazareth is that he existed. He was a real figure of history (we will consider later the historicity of the so-called infancy narratives). He was married to the greatest woman who ever lived. He was the virginal father of the man who was the human locus of the divine. Most important, he was the head of this unique family. He protected, provided for and guided God-with-us (Emmanuel) and the Mother of God. And yet of no one can it be said more truly that he put into practice what John the Baptist was later to declare: "He must increase, I must decrease."

(*John* 3:30). His whole life was centered on taking care of his extraordinary family – and when his mission came to an end and his Son came of age, he dropped out of sight. There the matter might have ended if Heaven had no other plans.

Now it is often said that we know very little about Joseph at least from the biblical texts. But even the little we know is rarely explored in the light of "the rest of the story." This is surely surprising given that the father played such a vital role in the life of the Son from his birth to those many years in which "he went down with them and came to Nazareth, and was obedient to them." (*Luke* 2:51). These were the years in which the Son of God made man "advanced (in) wisdom and age and favor before God and man." (2:52). Jesus was known in his "native place" as "the carpenter's son." (*Matthew* 13:55). In the Gospel of John he is referred to as "Jesus, the son of Joseph." (*John* 6:42). Who was the "carpenter?" What we know from the Gospels is that he was a man personally chosen and directed by God to protect the greatest treasure on earth with no special supernatural assistance beyond directives in dreams. This was a man trusted by God-in-Heaven. This was a man obeyed by God-with-us.

It should be noted that St. Joseph is the only prominent biblical figure of whom there are no recorded words. And yet, though we use words to communicate, words are not the only means of communication. Of St. Joseph well can we say that his actions themselves communicate a message that is stronger than anything he could have said in words. If the fundamental choice offered humanity is between obeying and disobeying God, then Joseph SHOWS us how to obey, an obedience that echoes the world-changing fiat of his Spouse and the supreme Sacrifice of his Son.

Role in the Salvific Scheme

But was his role in salvation history simply a one-time appearance? Instinctively we say "no." In the first place, when it came to the Incarnation, everything was planned. "For this I was born and for this I came into the world, to testify to the truth," said Jesus (*John* 18:37). He was "born" for a pre-existing purpose and therefore all circumstances surrounding his birth and his life were part of a divine blueprint. His mother had been chosen because she had found "favor with God" (*Luke* 1:30). She was "betrothed to a man named Joseph, of the house of David" (*Luke* 1:27) and thereby their Son could inherit "the throne of David his father" and thus he could "rule over the house of Jacob forever, and of his kingdom there will be no end." (32-33).

Hence Jesus could proclaim to Pilate that he was the sovereign of a celestial kingdom. Moreover, it was his father, "a righteous man" (*Matthew* 1:19), who was charged with revealing his salvific mission to the world. The archangel instructs him "you are to name him Jesus, because he will save his people from their sins" (*Matthew* 1:19) and obediently he "named him Jesus." (1:25).

On another level, no one has just a one-time appearance in salvation history. In the divine scheme of things, all beings – from the fallen angels to the heavenly hosts – are "put to work" until the end of time. And not only does Christ intercede endlessly before the heavenly Father ("he lives forever to make intercession for them" (*Hebrews* 7:25)) but the saints in Heaven continue their participation in God's plan on earth ("I saw underneath the altar the souls of those who had been slaughtered because of the witness they bore to the word of God. They cried out in a loud voice, 'How long will it be, holy and true master, before you sit in judgment and avenge our blood on the inhabitants of the earth?'" (*Revelation* 6:9-11).

As we on earth "persevere in running the race that lies before us", we are instructed to "rid ourselves of every burden and sin" by remembering that "we are surrounded by so great a cloud of witnesses." (*Hebrews* 12:1).

So how does this apply to *Saint* Joseph? From the apostolic age, the Christian world recognized that the Mother of the Messiah would continue to perform the mission she was given by the Archangel Gabriel until the end of history – she was the mother of all "those who keep God's commandments and bear witness to Jesus" (*Revelation* 12:17). The earliest Christian communities also took it as obvious that the Apostles and martyrs never ceased their intercession. This is evident from their prayers in the catacombs ("Peter and Paul pray for us," "O St. Sixtus, remember in your prayers Aurelius Repentinus," "Holy spirits, p(ray that) Verecundus may be safe at sea with his dear ones.") and in the ancient liturgies.

About Joseph, however, there is not much that we hear in these communities with one significant exception: in the heartland of ancient Christianity, the Copts, Greeks and Syrians kept alive the memory of the Guardian of the Redeemer.

We will see that an assemblage of "signs" led to the discovery of Joseph. These include Scripture, the tradition embodied in the work of the Doctors of the Church, the witness of the saints, theological development, the devotion of the faithful and the magisterium of the Church. But the first of the signs we consider are literally "signs" from Heaven.

Encounters with St. Joseph

For a good part of the impetus behind the new awareness of the Just Man (especially in the 19th and 20th centuries) came directly from Heaven. St. Joseph played a part in four of the most important approved Marian apparitions of the modern era.

He appeared along with Jesus, Mary and St. John the Evangelist at Knock, Ireland (1879) – as an indicator (it has been said) of his patronage of the Church throughout history. The significance of St. Joseph's appearance at Knock was specially recognized by the Church on the feast of St. Joseph in 2021 which had been declared the Year of St. Joseph. At Fatima, he was observed with the Baby Jesus during the miracle of the Sun "tracing the sign of the cross and appearing to bless the world." In a previous apparition, on September 13, 1917, Our Lady of Fatima prepared the visionaries for this appearance: "St Joseph will come with the Baby Jesus to give peace to the world." From this statement, it is obvious that St. Joseph is an integral part of the Triumph of the Immaculate Heart. The protector of the Holy Family now protects the world. At Akita, Japan (1973) – closely linked to Fatima – the angel warned the visionary of "difficult and numerous" obstacles and then reassured her with the words, "But St. Joseph will protect your work." He was seen again – this time by thousands of people – along with Jesus and Mary during the famous Zeitoun, Egypt apparitions of 1968. Separate from all this, at a personal level, St. Joseph appeared also to St. Faustina and such saints as St. Teresa of Avila.

A remarkable feature of the St. Joseph appearances is their congruence with the Gospel accounts. In Scripture, he is present as father and husband, guardian and provider. He is pointedly called "just." He freely and constantly follows divine direction. But, as we have noted, he is silent. The appearances of St. Joseph are also characterized by a similar silence. Moreover, for the most part these encounters take place in the context of the Holy Family.

Millennial Milestone

But where does all this take us? Only by apprehending him can we come to recognize the role of the Holy Family in human history.

On the one hand, we are simply following the trajectory of theological truth. Our fuller understanding of Jesus and Mary inevitably leads to an exploration into the person closest to them, the virginal father and husband. And here the theological momentum, devotional thrust, magisterial teaching and mystical manifestations of previous centuries seems to be moving to a climactic recognition of the role of St. Joseph. We are witnessing a prophetic drama unfolding before us.

On the second hand, as noted earlier, this is an age that calls for St, Joseph and his family. At a time like the present, when the miraculous institutions of marriage and the family, the fundamental units of society and humanity, are under relentless attack, the urgency of the finding of Joseph is especially apparent. For the Holy Family is both the perfect embodiment of marriage and family and an ever-present source of immediate assistance for all marriages and families and every parent and child.

With the loss of the father comes atheism. With the loss of the mother comes a hardness of heart. With the destruction of marriage as an institution we are left with the collapse of the family and the end of sanity. It is precisely in this perilous period that the Holy Family of Nazareth comes to the fore as the ark that will carry us across these troubled waters. But no understanding of the Holy Family is possible without an appreciation of the man who was husband and father.

Roadmap

Given our emphasis on the prophetic dimension, our study of St. Joseph must necessarily avail itself of a wide variety of resources.

The starting-point for the discovery of Joseph is his place in the story of Israel. In Joseph as in Mary his spouse, the history of the People of God converges toward its prophetic climax as the God of Abraham, Isaac and Jacob becomes "God with us". He is the bridge between the patriarchs of the Old Covenant and the Apostles of the New, the bearer of the line of David through whom the everlasting throne passes down to the King of All Nations, the fulcrum on which the sacred genealogy of Israel becomes the universal heritage of humanity.

From this launching-pad, we encounter a multitude of other dimensions, perspectives, insights: revelational, doctrinal, devotional, mystical, salvific, personal:

- ❖ the New Testament portrait of the just man.
- ❖ the eerie parallel between the Josephs of the Old and New Testaments.
- ❖ the recognition in the hearts and minds of the faithful that he who protected the Deus incarnatus and the Mater Dei from the forces of evil is the protector of all the faithful.

- ❖ the tomes and tracts of the mystics and saints who share pious visions of the hidden life of the Holy Family.
- ❖ the forceful papal pronouncements of the last century and a half affirming St. Joseph as protector and patron culminating in the declaration of 2020-21 as the Year of St. Joseph.
- ❖ the voice of Heaven that announces the true meaning of Joseph for the salvific plan of God in history.

All this, of course, leads to the profound and subtle truth unveiled by the great mystical doctors of Christian history – starting with St Teresa of Avila – that the Holy Family of Nazareth is a human mirror of the Divine Trinity and St. Joseph is the representative of the Father.

Before beginning our exploration, we should preempt myriad misconceptions by addressing two pivotal issues: what do we know about the historical Joseph? how can we talk of him as an intercessor for us today?

The first dimension in the discovery of Joseph is what we know of him historically. Here the normative source documents are the Gospel narratives and not the apocryphal accounts that sprang up centuries later. In these narratives we read about a man named Joseph who is betrothed to a young lady. The writers take great pains to point out that he is of royal descent and a "just man." Joseph undergoes a series of tests the first of which is his finding out that his betrothed is pregnant. This is followed by other traumatic trials: the birth of the child in a stable, a prophecy of suffering ahead for the child and his mother, the family's flight to a foreign land from a murderous despot, the "loss" of the son after a Temple pilgrimage. All these obstacles are overcome. And then Joseph vanishes without a trace from the Gospels (with the exception of brief references to Jesus as "the carpenter's son" and "the son of Joseph").

Despite the bare simplicity of the biblical narratives, there is buried within it a wealth of substance and meaning. There are also questions to be addressed:

- Are the infancy narratives historically accurate or a mythological accretion?
- Why are there inconsistencies in the genealogies of Matthew and Luke?
- Why are there apparent inconsistencies in the sequence of events narrated by Matthew and Luke?
- Did Joseph suspect Mary of infidelity?
- Did Joseph and Mary have other children?

- Was Joseph an old man who had children from a previous marriage.?

These concerns and questions will be addressed in our study of the Gospel passages.

A totally different issue arises when we consider Joseph as intercessor. There is, of course, the question of why he has been acclaimed as the greatest intercessor after the Blessed Virgin. More fundamental, however, is the critique that such elevation of a creature diminishes the glory of God. It is said that we can and should "go directly" to God without any mediator. Why do we need to pray to Mary or Joseph or any of the saints when we can go directly to Jesus as he himself exhorts: "Ask and it will be given to you; seek and you will find; knock and the door will be opened to you." (*Matthew* 7:7). This is the question that has puzzled and troubled all those who consider creaturely intercession and mediation. Often the answers given to these critiques and concerns do not engage the exact point of contention. It is not enough to say that the saints pray for us just as we pray for each other. The more basic question is this: why not go directly to God instead of going through other human persons?

And this is the question we will address at this introductory stage. The essential issue comes down to this: what is our understanding of the God revealed to us in Scripture and salvation history? Let us first consider two options that many Christians have chosen:

- On one extreme, there is the deist god who sets the universe in motion and then exits the scene: this god is not an Actor in human history. Everything in the world is done by creatures with no divine intervention of any kind.
- On the other extreme, there is the puppet-master god who not only creates the universe but orchestrates every event and the action of every creature in history: this god is the only Actor in human history. There is no creaturely intercession or mediation of any kind and we end up with a shadow variation of pantheism where everything is virtually a part of god.

Neither the people of Israel nor the early Church saw God in terms of either one of these extremes. Rather the biblical God was omnipotent, omniscient and all-good, on the one hand, but also, on the other, the Creator of free beings who are given the choice of either cooperating with or rejecting the divine will. These free beings, moreover, were given the responsibility for working with each other in families and communities that would help guide their members to union with the divine Will. Every choice has a consequence – good or bad – and these consequences are shared by families, communities and all of humanity. Most important, those who chose to become members of the family of God could, should and would help other members of the family: this indeed is what mediation is all about rather than some abstract theory about intermediaries.

Take the people of Israel and the coming of Jesus. Without the cooperation of Abraham, Moses, David and the Prophets and Law-givers, the Incarnation of God in Jesus Christ would not have been possible. Likewise, without the cooperation and mediation of the Apostles and the other disciples, and of Fathers, Councils, Popes, priests, evangelists and others there would have been no propagation of Jesus' message of salvation, no formulation of the doctrines revealed by God, no continued performance of the actions commanded in the Gospels such as baptism. Historically, then, intercession and mediation were fundamental to the revelation of God through the people of Israel and finally in and through Jesus of Nazareth.

Intercession and mediation are, in fact, essentially embedded in the incarnation of God in Christ. Consider just two of Jesus' statements: "I tell you the truth, whatever you did not do for one of the least among you, you did not do for me." (*Matthew* 25:41-45). "Saul, Saul, why do you persecute me?" (*Acts* 9:4). Once we take these two statements seriously we realize that the Incarnation makes every human person a vital participant in the drama of salvation. Jesus identifies himself with the least among us and with his Church. Our free acts either help or hurt him. Every choice we make is for or against Jesus and only we can make that choice. We are offered the opportunity to be mediators of Jesus' love.

But the mediation of Joseph and Mary is of a different order from the followers of the Risen Jesus. Unlike all other human persons, Joseph and Mary were intimate participants in the mystery of the Incarnation from its very beginning. Mary is the New Eve and hers is a maternal mediation that is unique. St. Joseph' mediation is likewise unique, rooted as it is in his role in the Holy Family as husband and father. Moreover, it has been well argued that the Holy Family mirrors, albeit remotely, the Holy Trinity. Because the Holy Family played a unique role in salvation history, it belongs to a different dimension of "action" from all other agents.

Three Dimensions of Revelation and Mediation

This needs clarification. There are three dimensions of action or modes of interaction with the divine in salvation history.

- First, the dimension of action of Preparatory Revelation, Transitional Mediation and Prophecy. This structure underlies the world of the Old Testament.
- This is followed by the dimension of action of Incarnation, Redemption and Ultimate Mediation that we find in the Gospels.
- Finally, there is the dimension of action of disseminating the message of salvation and dispensing the means of sanctification that unfolds in the Acts of the Apostles, the New Testament Epistles and the history of the Church.

At the center of the dimension of Incarnation, Redemption and Ultimate Mediation is the incarnate Word of God who is Redeemer and infinite Mediator. But united with him, GIVEN by him and working with him in a unique and irrevocable mode is his mother and his earthly father. The mother is the New Eve, the Mother of all Christians and the Mother of the Church. The father is the Protector, the Guide and the spiritual father of all the faithful.

To the extent that the Redeemer is a man who is irreversibly united to a divine nature, he is the Son of Joseph and Mary. To the extent that his freely willed redemptive death was a human act, albeit the human act of a divine Person, it was an act that drew on the cooperation of two human persons, Joseph and Mary. To the extent that the mediation of the fruits of the redemptive act calls on the participation of human agents in the mediation of the One Primary Mediator, Joseph and Mary exercise a unique form of such participation: Mary's maternal mediation for the brothers and sisters of her Son and Joseph's mediation as head of the Holy Family. Above all, Joseph and Mary are gifts of their Son to the faithful.

To take up what was said earlier, the role of Joseph and Mary in the mission of Jesus cannot possibly be thought to have ended with their deaths. For Jesus as a human being lives forever and they will forever be father and mother of God incarnate. Just as important, in their lives on earth and forever after, this family of Nazareth is a likeness of the Holy Trinity – Joseph as representative of the Father, Jesus as literally the Son and Mary as the image of the Holy Spirit. Moreover, they continue to play a part in human history: not only was the Holy Family the beginning of the Christian Church but, as *Revelation* 12:17 indicates, the Mother of God is the mother of all Christians and, that being the case, her husband is the spiritual earthly father of the very same Christians. They draw us into their family, the family of God. "So then you are no longer strangers and sojourners, but you are fellow citizens with the holy ones and members of the household of God." (*Ephesians* 2:19).

The voyage of discovery culminating in St. Joseph and the Holy Family is graphically represented below. What lies behind this sequence of discoveries? And what are the implications of the discoveries? It is this that we propose to explore here.

- Discovery of Joseph
- Discovery of the Holy Family
- Discovery of the Holy Family as the model for all families
- Discovery of the Holy Family as a family we are called to enter
- Discovery of the Holy Family as the earthly representative of the Holy Trinity
- Discovery of the Holy Family as the key to becoming part of God's family
- Discovery of the role of the Holy Family in the world and in human history

We will say more as we proceed but it should be apparent at this stage that the new appreciation for the universal patronage and protection of St. Joseph – in terms of both doctrine and devotion – is organically rooted in the dynamic of salvation history.

The Seven Signs

To sum up, to discover Joseph is to recognize his prophetic role in our day. He is the man of the millennium because he is the final horizon of a journey that began at and through the junction of B.C. and A.D. In every age since the explosion of infinite Love that was the Incarnation, we move forward by peering backward. And today, with such sophisticated theological telescopes as contemplative study, centuries-spanning prayer and divinely guided discernment, we see "the third man" at Ground Zero as Guardian of the human family, patron of the Church of God, shadow of the Father. This is what the signs tell us. This is the message of Heaven.

As it relates to Joseph of Nazareth, we might say there are seven signs in all, seven streams that come together to consummate the ensemble of revelation, incarnation and salvation. They are:

- the Voice of Heaven as manifested in history
- the scriptural starting points
- the testimony of Tradition
- the case laid out by the saints
- the blossoming of ancient theological buds
- the personal experience of the faithful
- the proclamation of the Church

Singly and collectively, they compel us to consider the role of the "just man" in the salvific scheme as it relates to humanity and our own lives. Accordingly, we will now work our way through each one of these singular "sign"-posts on the highway to Heaven.

Heaven has spoken – Encounters of the Third Order

The history of Christianity has been marked by an abundance of supernatural phenomena. that were as unique as they were influential. Among these phenomena, the most dramatic are reports of encounters with Jesus and Mary, dramatic not simply as phenomena in themselves but for the content of the associated messages and the impact of these encounters on subsequent history. Each of these two types of encounters – those with Jesus and those with Mary – had their own characteristic patterns.

Both types are introduced in the New Testament with Saul's vision of the Risen Christ (*Acts of the Apostles* 9) and St. John's account of the Woman Clothed with the Sun (*Revelation* 12). Thenceforth they are found in virtually every century and across the world. Marian apparitions, starting with St. James in the first century and ranging from France and Mexico to India, Rwanda and Vietnam, combine messages and public signs: repentance, consecration, prophecies, healing springs, miraculous objects like the tilma image of Guadalupe. Visions of Jesus, beginning with one witnessed by Pope Alexander I in 118, are best known for their accompanying messages, most famously those of the Sacred Heart and the Divine Mercy, and center on a deeper understanding of the Incarnation and its implications for everyday life. A vision is a spiritual manifestation to a selected person whereas an apparition is a flesh-and-blood appearance that engages the sensory organs of one or more recipients and often includes publicly visible "signs" such as a healing spring. The common theme in both types of encounter is conversion and transformation.

A third and more recent kind of encounter, what we might call a "third order" of celestial appearances, involves the third member of the Holy Family, Joseph of Nazareth. These encounters, certified after investigation by the Church as "worthy of belief," began in earnest in the nineteenth century (although St. Joseph had a much older "French connection" dating back to the sixteenth and seventeenth centuries). The third differs from the first and the second orders of appearances in three salient respects: Joseph appears with the two other members of his family; for the most part, he appears but does not speak (although in one instance he acts, blessing the world); and there is an implicit backdrop of danger against which he appears.

So why these appearances of St. Joseph and why now? These are the questions we will consider here and there is no better place to start than the appearances themselves.

Knock, Ireland

The first major encounter with St. Joseph was reported in Knock, Ireland, in August 21, 1879. Knock, the Gaelic word for "hill," was a poverty-stricken town in the west of Ireland. Here, for over two hours on a rainy night, three men, six women, two teenage boys and a girl, and two children, witnessed a heavenly tableau outside the gable of the local Church. In the midst of a bright light stood the Blessed Virgin Mary along with St. Joseph and St. John the Evangelist, author of the Book of Revelation. Behind them on a altar with a cross rested a Lamb surrounded by angels.

In the words of the witnesses, here is what took place:

Mary Beirne (twenty six years old at the time) [1]:

> "At the distance of three hundred yards or so from the church, I beheld all at once, standing out from the gable, and rather to the west of it, three figures which, on more attentive inspection, appeared to be that of the Blessed Virgin, of St. Joseph, and St. John. That of

the Blessed Virgin was life-size, the others apparently either not so big or not so high as her figure; they stood a little distance out from the gable wall, and as well as I could judge, a foot and a half or two from the ground.

"The Virgin stood erect, with eyes raised to heaven, her hands elevated to the shoulders or a little higher, the palms inclined slightly toward the shoulders or bosom; she wore a large cloak of a white color, hanging in full folds and somewhat loosely around her shoulders and fastened to the neck; she wore a crown on the head - a rather large crown - and it appeared to be somewhat yellower than the dress or robes worn by Our Blessed Lady.

"In the figure of St. Joseph, the head was slightly bent, and inclined toward the Blessed Virgin, as if paying her respect; it represented the saint somewhat aged with gray whiskers and grayish hair. The third figure appeared to be that of St. John the Evangelist; I do not know, only I thought so, except the fact that at one time I saw a statue [of St. John] at the chapel of Lekanvey, near Westport, County Mayo, very much resembling the figure which now stood before me.

"Above the altar, and resting on it was a lamb, standing with face toward St. John, thus fronting the western sky. I saw no cross or crucifix. On the body of the lamb and around it, I saw golden stars, or small brilliant lights, glittering like jets or glass balls, reflecting the light of some luminous body.

"I remained from a quarter past eight to half past nine o'clock."

Patrick Hill (eleven years old at the time) [2]:

> I saw St. Joseph to the Blessed Virgin's right hand; his head was bent from the shoulders, forward; he appeared to be paying his respects; I noticed his whiskers; they appeared slightly gray; there was line or dark mearing [Western term for division, as between farms or townlands] between the figure of the Blessed Virgin and that of St. Joseph, so that one could know St. Joseph, and the place where his figure appeared distinctly from that of the Blessed Virgin and the spot where she stood. I saw the feet of St. Joseph, too; his hands were joined like a person at prayer.

Bridget Trench (seventy five years old at the time)[3]:

> I was so taken with the Blessed Virgin that I did not pay much attention to any other; yet I saw also the two other figures -- St. Joseph standing to the right of the Blessed Virgin, or to the left, as I looked at him, his head bent towards her and his hands joined; and the other figure, which I took to be St. John the Evangelist, was standing at her left. I heard those around me say that the image was St. John.

Soon after the apparition, people with ailments reported being cured after visits to Knock. In fact within the first year after the apparition, over 300 people announced to the parish priest that they had been cured of one ailment or another. Two commissions of inquiry were appointed by Church authorities, first in 1879 and yet again in 1936 to investigate the purported apparition. Both commissions concluded that the witnesses were trustworthy. Knock is today one of modern Europe's major pilgrimage destinations.

Although the apparition took place in 1879, the fullest recognition of its supernaturality by the Vatican took place only in 2021. On the feast of St. Joseph, March 19, in the Year of St. Joseph, 2021, Pope Francis declared Knock an International

Marian and Eucharistic Shrine. This was the date chosen specifically because of St. Joseph's appearance at Knock.

Fatima, Portugal

Fatima is the most famous Marian apparition of the twentieth century especially given its relevance for subsequent world events. But not many realize that this apparition also involved St. Joseph.

The Blessed Virgin appeared on six different occasions to three peasant children in Fatima, Portugal in 1917. Among other things, they were given a vision of Hell. On October 13, the day of the final apparition, 70,000 people people saw the sun spinning on its axis and hurtling toward the earth before returning to its normal position. After 13 years of investigation, the Bishop of Leiria declared the apparitions of Fatima worthy of belief in October 1930.

Fatima is just as well known for its Secrets (particularly the Third Secret which spoke of the assassination of a Pope) and its prophetic perspective on world events. The Virgin warned that a greater war than the last one (i.e., the First World War) would break out under the next pontificate if people did not stop offending God. When an unknown light illumined the night, it would be a sign of this impending war. This illumination did take place before the Second World War. She also asked for a consecration of Russia to her Immaculate Heart by the Pope and acts of reparation on First Saturdays. If this were not done, Russia would spread its errors and entire nations would be annihilated. Yet in the end her Immaculate Heart would triumph because the Pope would consecrate Russia to her and the country would be converted followed by a short time of peace. Although most people thought this prophecy to be fanciful, Fatima devotees continued to say the Rosary for the conversion of Russia. Finally, on March 25, 1984, Pope John Paul II consecrated Russia and the world to the Immaculate Heart as a direct response to the Virgin's request. In early 1989, Sister Lucia sent a communication to the world announcing that the Pope's consecration had been accepted by God and that its results would become apparent later that year. In late 1989 the Berlin Wall had fallen and by August of 1991 Russia was no longer Communist.

In the September 13th apparition, the Virgin had said that in October she would be accompanied by St. Joseph and the Child Jesus. The visionaries witnessed the appearance of the Holy Family during the October "miracle of the sun." Said Sister Lucia, "After Our Lady had disappeared into the immense distance of the firmament, we beheld St. Joseph with the Child Jesus and Our Lady robed in white with a blue mantle, beside the sun. St. Joseph and the Child Jesus appeared to bless the world, for they traced the Sign of the Cross with their hands."[4]

Zeitoun, Egypt

As the Gospels have it, the Holy Family of Nazareth had fled to Egypt to escape Herod's persecution. For centuries, many places in Egypt are associated with their onward and return journeys. One such was said to be the city of Mataria today known as Zeitoun. A church called St. Mary's was built on the very place where the Family had lived during their Egyptian visitation. The church disappeared and was rebuilt several times until by 1918 it came into the possession of a Coptic Christian family. In that year it was reported that the Virgin Mary told the member of this family that the site was important for her. Moreover, in fifty years she would bestow a special blessing on a church to be built there. The family gave the land to the Coptic Church who built there another church of St. Mary.

Fifty years later, in 1968, it was here that the Virgin Mary appeared to a million people and more over several months starting on the 2nd of April. Witnesses included Moslems, Jews and Christians and even the then President of Egypt. The apparitions were broadcast on Egyptian TV and filmed by numerous professional photographers. Miracles of all kinds were reported. Never before was an apparition of the Virgin witnessed by so many – and not just once but over a lengthy period of time. After extensive investigation, both the Coptic Orthodox Church and the Catholic Church affirmed this apparition to be worthy of belief.

Here is a brief description from the official announcement of the Coptic authorities[5]:

> Since the evening of Tuesday April 2, 1968 (the 24th of Bramhat, 1684 A.M.), the apparitions of the Holy Virgin Saint Mary, Mother of Light, have continued in the Coptic Orthodox Church named after Her in Zeitoun, Cairo.
>
> The apparitions occurred on many different nights and are continuing in different forms. The Holy Virgin Saint Mary appeared sometimes in full form and sometimes in a bust, surrounded with a halo of shining light. She was seen at times on the openings of the domes on the roof of the church, and at other times outside the domes, moving and walking on the roof of the church and over the domes. When She knelt in reverence in front of the cross, the cross shone

with bright light. Waving Her blessed hands and nodding Her holy head, She blessed the people who gathered to observe the miracle. She appeared sometimes in the form of a body like a very bright cloud, and sometimes as a figure of light preceded with heavenly bodies shaped like doves moving at high speeds. The apparitions continued for long periods, up to 2 hours and 15 minutes as in the dawn of Tuesday April 30, 1968 (the 22nd of Barmouda, 1684 A.M.), when She appeared continuously from 2:45 am till 5:00 am.

One dimension of these apparitions is of special interest in the current context. It did not include just the Virgin: "Sometimes, along with doves and angels, meteors and strange lights, She has been seen in the company of Her beloved Joseph, Her Sacred Child, and even a lowly little burro."[6] Or, as another report put it, "On some evenings the Blessed Mother is accompanied by Saint Joseph and the Infant Jesus."

Akita, Japan

The next relevant apparition does not involve an appearance by St. Joseph but a message concerning his significance. Akita, Japan is where the Virgin Mary spoke to a nun, Agnes Sasagawa, in 1973 through a miraculous statue that wept and bled even on Japanese national TV. The bleeding came from a cross-shaped wound on the palm of the right hand. The apparition was approved as authentic by the local bishop John Ito in 1981. Although other Japanese bishops were later critical of Akita, their knowledge of the matter was tangential. Bishop Ito was the bishop in charge at the time of the apparitions and, what is more, he had personally witnessed four of the Akita miracles. He declared, "I recognize the supernatural character of a series of mysterious events concerning the statue of the Holy Mother Mary which is found in the convent of the Institute of the Handmaids of the Sacred Heart of Jesus in the Holy Eucharist at Yuzawadai, Soegawa, Akita. I do not find in these events any elements which are contrary to Catholic faith and morals."[7]

Remarkably, the 2011 Japanese tsunami is connected to Akita: "The epicenter of the earthquake that caused a deadly March 11 tsunami is located near the site of an apparition in which Mary warned about a worldwide disaster that could afflict humanity."[8] This kind of connection is not unusual: Mary appeared in Kibeho in Rwanda warning of impending calamity prior to its descent into genocide. She appeared in two Belgian towns, Beauraing and Banneux, located in the Ardennes in 1932 and 1933 grave and sorrowful. It was here that the most destructive battle of the Second World War, the Battle of the Bulge, took place.

The best known message of Akita was the last one delivered on October 13, the anniversary of the last Fatima apparition:

> My dear daughter, listen well to what I have to say to you. And relay my messages to your superior.
>
> As I told you, if men do not repent and better themselves, the Heavenly Father will inflict a great punishment on all humanity. It will definitely be a punishment greater than the Deluge, such as has never been seen before.
>
> Fire will plunge from the sky and a large part of humanity will perish ... The good as well as the bad will perish, sparing neither priests nor the faithful. The survivors will find themselves plunged into such terrible hardships that they will envy the dead. The only arms which will remain for you will be the Rosary and the sign left by My Son (Eucharist).
>
> Each day recite the prayers of the Rosary. With the Rosary pray for the bishops and priests. The work of the devil will infiltrate even into the Church. One will see cardinals opposing

other cardinals, and bishops confronting other bishops.[9]

As with the children at Fatima, Sister Agnes had angelic guidance in her encounters. It is from her guardian angel that Agnes heard about St. Joseph. When Agnes' community prayed for the protection of St. Joseph for their work of furthering belief in the Eucharistic Presence of Jesus, the angel told her: "This prayer is very pleasing to Jesus and Mary. It will be heard … [But] It is sad that there is no exterior sign here in honor of Saint Joseph. Ask your superior to have an exterior sign erected in his honor when you are able."[10] The angel said that the more they try to perform the task given by the Blessed Virgin "the more difficult and numerous will be the obstacles. But St. Joseph will protect your work." Thus, at Akita, St. Joseph is called on to protect apostolic work involving Jesus and Mary.

Reading Between the Signs

So what is the moral of these stories? What is Heaven trying to tell us? In pondering these questions, we would do well to consider not simply the actual encounters but their raison d etre and then the themes they embody and finally their implications for the future. Only this can help us understand their meaning and significance in its entirety.

When we say "raison d etre" we are talking about the question of whether or not there was a reason why a particular apparition took place where and when it did. For there is a cause-and-effect sequence in the spiritual world that is as real as the causal sequence in the physical realm. In the biblical narratives, for instance, we see that the primordial rejection of the divine will had cascading catastrophic consequences for subsequent history just as Abraham's obedience to God redounded to the well-being of his progeny.

With respect to the apparitions, we have already seen that the Zeitoun apparitions took place at the precise location where the Holy Family is traditionally believed to have stayed. As for Knock, St. Patrick, the Apostle of Ireland, had apparently blessed this little hamlet and prophesied that it would become a great pilgrimage site for millions. In the apparition at Knock, "Mary wore a beautiful rose, which foreshadowed her later coming at Fatima as Our Lady of the Rosary. Along with St. John the Evangelist, St. Joseph's presence at Knock that night is believed to have been a mighty indicator of his universal patronage of the Church throughout history and especially now."[11]

Fatima's history is directly linked to that of Portugal and to a twentieth century papal request for an intervention from Heaven. First, in 1646, after winning victories against vastly superior armies, King John IV of Portugal offered his crown to Our Lady of the Immaculate Conception and then declared her the Patroness of Portugal. No king of Portugal since then wore a crown. Fatima, named after a Moslem princess who had become a Catholic, was itself a supernaturally significant venue. General Nuno Alvares Pereira, an ancestor of John IV, led the Portuguese to victory against the Castilian army at the Battle of Aljubarotta in 1385. On the eve of the battle, Nuno "asked for a sign from God that his greatly outnumbered army would be victorious through the intercession of 'Our Lady Queen of Portugal.' When the advancing troops arrived at the Cova da Iria of Fatima, the horses began to kneel and Nuno was led to a place upon the Mount of Saint Michael where the apparitions of Fatima occurred in 1917."[12]

Here, Nuno "was reportedly told the ground he knelt on was holy and that one day God bring victory over evil on this very spot and an era of peace would be granted to the world."[13] Nuno's victory – aided it is said, by apparitions to the soldiers of St. Michael and the Blessed Virgin – had significant consequences: "Nuno achieved his victory the next day, opening the way, even historians concur, for the great evangelization and exploration of the new world that would arise from Portugal because of this significant event."[14] After the victory, at the request of the King of Portugal, Pope Boniface IX, on May 13, decreed that all the Cathedrals in Portugal should be dedicated to the Virgin Mary: not by coincidence, the first apparition of Fatima took place on May 13 several centuries later.

The twentieth century Fatima apparition was in some respects a direct response to a plea from Pope Benedict XV who implored the intercession of the Blessed Mother in bringing the Great War of 1914 to a halt. On May 5, 1917, the Pope sent out a pastoral letter to the world in which he asked the faithful to petition Mary the Mother of Mercy in "this awful hour" "that her most tender and benign solicitude may be moved and the peace we ask for be obtained for our agitated world." Within eight days, on the 13th of May, the Mother of Mercy appeared at Fatima with her own "peace plan" for the world. Incidentally, in the third of the Fatima apparitions, the Virgin said that the present war would come to an end (something that most people found unbelievable at the time) but a new and greater war would begin during the papacy of Pius XI. At Fatima, the Blessed Mother had said, "she would bring St. Joseph with the Holy Child 'to bless the world and bring it peace.'"[15] With his presence in the final apparition, "at Fatima, God left no doubt that St. Joseph was an important part of His plan to convert the world through the Immaculate Heart of Mary."[16]

The Akita apparition is "connected" to Fatima in multiple ways. Like Fatima, the Akita message was prayer, penance, reparation for sins. If Fatima showed the fiery flames of Hell as the ultimate consequence of sin, the warning of Akita is that the sins of the world are going to call down fire from the sky which will destroy much of humanity. Of course, the final message of Akita took place on the same date as the final apparition of Fatima (October 13).

John Haffert, the founder of the Fatima apostolate, the Blue Army, notes seven other parallels: both at Akita and Fatima, a statue of the Virgin came to life and the Pilgrim Virgin of Fatima has shed tears like the Akita statue of Our Lady of All Nations; an angel taught Sister Agnes the same prayer that was taught at Fatima; at both Fatima and Akita, angels prepared the visionaries for the coming of the Virgin; Eucharistic miracles preceded both Fatima and Akita; the Real Presence of Christ in the Eucharist was strongly affirmed in both apparitions; both stressed the importance of praying the Rosary; the Fatima and Akita messages include the observation that only the Virgin's intercession can save the faithful from certain chastisements. And, of course, both point to the role of St. Joseph.

Haffert goes further on the St. Joseph connection at Fatima and Akita: "At the same time a third heart emerges from the drama and light both of AKITA and Fatima. It is the chaste heart of St. Joseph. He appeared with the Holy Child in the sky of Fatima during the great miracle to bless the world and "bring it peace." At Akita Our Lady said that in the great battle now being waged by Satan and his legions, the apostles of the Two Hearts would be the object of their special hatred but that, "Saint Joseph will protect your work." We are stressing this at some length in these pages because very little has been said about the role of St. Joseph. Why is St. Joseph given as the protector of this apostolate to save the world from a terrible chastisement? St. Joseph was the protector of the Two Hearts in life. He was the Protector of the Immaculate Heart of Mary and to the Sacred Heart beating in Her Virginal womb... the Sacred Heart of Incarnate Love. Is it not fitting that now when Our Lady comes to announce the triumph of Her Immaculate Heart, which will be the triumph of the Sacred Heart of Jesus, that St. Joseph again should be the Protector?"[17]

Historically, the devotion to St. Joseph and the Holy Family were introduced from the beginning and fervently developed in the New World by the French, Spanish and Portuguese missionaries. St. Joseph was declared the patron saint of both New Spain and New France.

"It might be expected that veneration of St. Joseph and the Holy Family in the New World lagged behind initiatives promoting these devotions in Europe. On the contrary, these devotions took canonical and liturgical forms in New Spain (present-day Mexico, Central America, and the Philippines) and New France (all the possessions of France in North America – an immense territory extending from present-day Canada to the Gulf of Mexico) that anticipated by several decades their evolution in the Old World…. Official ecclesiastical approbation of the great devotion and veneration accorded by St. Joseph by all the faithful, Amerindians and Spaniards alike, occurred very early in the history of New Spain…. St. Joseph's feast day was a holy day of obligation – sixty-six years before Pope Gregory XV (reigned 1621-1623) so designated it for the Universal Church in 1621…. In New Spain, the parents of Jesus also became the parents of the Amerindians."[18]

Dreamer and Doer – the Biblical Story

It is sometimes said that doctrines and devotions relating to St. Joseph have been built out of thin air since the Scriptures say almost nothing about him. But this opinion is mistaken at several levels and never more so than when it appeals to the silence of Scripture. In point of fact, what is astonishing is the failure to plumb the depths of all that is said about Joseph in the Gospels. Sacred Scripture, in fact, calls out for a doctrinal and devotional response that has yet to be fully answered!

Here is the vision of Joseph laid out in Holy Writ:

1. He is intimately linked to God's great covenants in salvation history, with the great mediators ranging from Abraham to Moses to David. On another level he is linked with the very origins of humanity – with a family tree going back to Adam. No one else in the Bible has merited this bi-focal treatment. We know, of course, that this chain is revealed precisely because it culminates in Jesus the Christ, the new Adam, the seed of Abraham in whom all humanity is blessed. But we forget that there had to be a bridge between

the covenants and this bridge was none other than Joseph.
2. He was a "just" man – in short, he was a canonized saint before there were canonized saints.
3. He was chosen and directed by God.
4. He protected and provided for his spouse and Son in terms of their physical needs and participated in performing their obligations before God (the circumcision, the naming, the presentation at the Temple). Together the three constituted a family, *his* family. This was a true family because he was a true husband and a true father (both of which were terms used to describe him)
5. His Son was "subject" to him and his wife as long as he (Joseph) was alive.
6. He taught his Son his trade and shared with him the salvific history of the Hebraic people.
7. He and his spouse had an unprecedented role in the ministry of the only begotten Son of God because it fell to them and only them to prepare the Man Who was God for his redemptive mission. Moreover, Mary's unique "Yes" and Joseph's unwavering obedience set the stage for the salvific Sacrifice of their beloved Son. The Redeemer was born into and nurtured by a family. This remains his

family. And because of its pivotal role in the salvific scheme, it is a family that serves as a model for all of humanity while enjoining all to become a part of it.

All this we saw because it was right before us in the scriptural record. We saw but did not notice. Hence this book.

The problem we face is not a deficit of information about Joseph in the biblical records but a glut of disinformation purveyed by non-biblical sources. Before we consider the latter let us note that Scripture tells us three central truths about Joseph that constitute his true glory:

- he is always and immediately obedient to God;
- he is the husband of the Mother of God;
- his covenantal union with Mary makes him the true father of their virginal Son.

The divine Logos not only took on human nature through a human being but his incarnation was inextricably and indissolubly embedded in a human family. Jesus, Mary and Joseph were, are and will always be the First Family of humanity.

Instead of pondering the meaning and mystery of these three great revealed truths about Joseph we have either bemoaned the absence of irrelevant material or fabricated apocryphal fantasies. We "strain out the gnat and swallow the camel!" We have missed not simply the forest but the trees as well.

So it's time to get back to basics. All later doctrine and devotion pertaining to Joseph has to be rooted in what we read in the biblical texts because this is the "public revelation" pertaining to him Indeed we find that all of Josephology, like all of Mariology, finds its starting-point and directional horizon in Scripture. But to study Scripture is to discover its depths and discern its multifold messaging. And this can only happen if we are guided in our study by what Scripture itself calls the "pillar and foundation of truth" (1 *Timothy* 3:15) – the Church.

The process of "unpacking" what is hidden in plain sight takes time. Only after we have recognized all dimensions of the personhood and mission of the Son and his Virgin Mother can we grasp the significance of the faithful spouse and virginal father. Only after we have been bequeathed the treasury of revealed truth that are the divine Trinity and the two natures of Christ can we see more clearly the blueprint behind the Incarnation. This kind of unpacking emerged and emerges only over centuries. The literalist who today condemns alleged new "unbiblical" inventions about Joseph has the same mind-set as the Arian (ancient or contemporary) who denies the divinity of Jesus on the basis of certain Scriptural texts or the Pneumatomachian who, again citing the Bible, holds that the Holy Spirit is a creation of God. Those who appeal to "biblical truths" often have no idea that the "truths" with which they are familiar (such as the Trinity or the two natures) were not spelled out in so many words in Scripture. Rather it was the Church, inspired by the Holy Spirit, and in the face of opposition from many devout Christians, that pronounced authoritatively on these matters – over centuries. As if to make this same point, many groups that have sprung up in the present day have built their beliefs around their own reading of Scripture and have ended up with non-Trinitarian theologies. To ignore salvation history in the name of "biblical truth" is to end up embracing beliefs that have long been condemned as unbiblical.

The development in our understanding of St. Joseph and his role, then, comes from deeper reflection on the portrait we are given in Scripture and in the light of Christian truth as a whole. It is in this context that we consider the assumptions and implications of the familiar facts: his spousal union; his being "just"; his protection of his unique family; his direct divine direction; his tutelage of his Son. The more we grasp the mystery of the divinity of Jesus the more we marvel at the glory of his humanity. The more we learn about Jesus being the Son of the Most High the more we learn about his being the Son of Adam and the Son of Abraham via his virginal father. The more we reflect on the covenantal structure of marriage and family, the more we appreciate the significance of Jesus' family.

Father

Let us consider this last theme. Jesus is a fruit of the marriage of Joseph and Mary. He was born to a married couple, Joseph and Mary, and so he is THEIR Son. The common misconception that Joseph and Mary were simply "engaged" and not married reflects ignorance of the Jewish practices of the day.

Fr. Richard Foley points out that: "The Messiah's parents-to-be would have followed scrupulously the conventional procedures laid down by Jewish law and custom as regards getting married. The ceremonies involved were performed in two stages, the first of which, known as espousals, was in fact the operative factor in that it effectively made the couple husband and wife. Far from simply amounting to what we would call their engagement, a true and valid marriage was contracted when, at this first stage, the partners plighted their troth and exchanged conjugal rights. The second stage of the marriage ceremony was its public celebration or solemnization…. Stage two of the marriage ceremony was purely social in effect, its central feature being the bride's induction into her husband's home."

Clearly the circumstances of Jesus' birth were unique. Every human soul is a direct creation of God. But the human person is a union of body and soul. Since there can be no body without a soul and since the matter that makes up the body comes from both parents, the human person is a fruit of the cooperation between God and two human beings. The person is human because the parents are human. The human person emerges from the partnership between these two human beings, on one hand, and God who is the Source of the animating principle or soul, a principle that in human beings has both intellect and will.

But Jesus was not a human person. He was a "divine Person," one of the Three hypostases or Ways of Existing of the Infinite-Eternal. He was the Logos, the Second Person of the Trinity, uniting himself with a human body and soul. Three things should be noted about this uniting of a divine Person with a human nature:

(a) the divine Person always existed and was not brought into being by Mary just as his divine Nature was not in any sense dependent on her;

(b) since he was not a human person, his taking on "human being" did not require the cooperation of two parents with God – in particular the generative action of a father. God, of course, directly created his human soul (as in the case of every human being). His body he received entirely from Mary.

(c) Mary was truly the mother of the divine Person in his union with a human body and soul: this Jesus who was a unique union of divine Person and human nature was truly a human being and every human being has a human parent.

This brings us to Joseph. Now though he was not the physical progenitor of Jesus, Joseph was truly his father: he had entered into the divinely instituted covenant of marriage with Mary and was therefore spiritually and morally one with her (as *Genesis* puts it, in marriage "the two of them become one body." 2:24): it is while they were married that Mary conceived and gave birth to Jesus.

The conception and birth was necessarily miraculous because the act of Incarnation could not be driven by any human agency: the Word became flesh and not the other way round. Nevertheless, the Incarnation took place within the covenantal unity of husband

and wife and God incarnate was therefore the son of a father and a mother. Mary was physically and spiritually the mother of Jesus while Joseph was the covenantal and virginal father of Jesus.

The Gospels clearly specify that Joseph and Mary are husband and wife and call Joseph the "father" of Jesus. As Fr. Joseph Lienhard has pointed out, St. Augustine shows why these descriptions are wholly appropriate.

> "Augustine develops at length his teaching that Joseph and Mary contracted a true marriage. He writes in Sermon 51, "Joseph then was not the less his father, because he knew not the mother of our Lord, as though concupiscence and not conjugal love (caritas coniugalis) constituted the marriage bond." What makes a woman a wife, he writes is not lust (libido) but conjugal love. Augustine demonstrates his point with two arguments, one positive and the other negative. Positively, if a couple follows Paul's advice and abstains from relations (1 Cor 7:29), they do not cease to be husband and wife; by mutual agreement they restrain the concupiscence of the flesh but not conjugal love. Negatively, a man who commits fornication does not thereby contract marriage, whereas a chaste man and woman are husband and wife "because there

is no fleshly intercourse, but only the union of hearts between them." …

In two other works, *On Marriage and Concupiscence* and *Against Julian*, Augustine defined the three goods of marriage: fidelity, which prevents adultery; offspring; and the sacramental bond, because there is no divorce. All three goods, he writes, are fulfilled in the parents of Christ.

Thus Augustine, like Ambrose, by drawing on the understanding of marriage from Roman law, can give an account of the marriage of Mary and Joseph as a true marriage and offer an understanding of marriage that finds its essence in a relationship between two persons rather than in corporeal intercourse. The high point of Augustine's teaching is his assertion that a marriage is constituted by conjugal love (*caritas coniugalis*), an idea that Roman law could never have proposed. (21, 24).[2]

Augustine was also emphatic that Joseph was the father of Jesus. "He devotes one third of Sermon 51 to defending Joseph's true fatherhood of Jesus. Since he clearly affirms Mary's perpetual virginity and thus her virginal conception of Jesus, he proposes an understanding of fatherhood that is not merely physical or corporeal. The essence of fatherhood, he will write, consists not in the act of begetting but rather in a relationship between a man and his son. In his affirmation of Joseph's true fatherhood, Augustine begins from Scripture, where Luke twice writes of Joseph as Jesus' father.... When he asks what constitutes true fatherhood, Augustine has three answers: paternal authority, natural affection; and marital fidelity, love and affection."[3]

John Paul II reaffirms Joseph's unique fatherhood:

> As can be deduced from the gospel texts, Joseph's marriage to Mary is the juridical basis of his fatherhood. It was to assure fatherly protection for Jesus that God chose Joseph to be Mary's spouse. It follows that Joseph's fatherhood—a relationship that places him as close as possible to Christ, to whom every election and predestination is ordered (cf. Rom 8:28-29)—comes to pass through marriage to Mary, that is, through the family.
>
> While clearly affirming that Jesus was conceived by the power of the Holy Spirit, and that virginity remained intact in the marriage (cf. Mt 1:18-25; Lk 1:26-38), the evangelists refer to Joseph as Mary's husband and to Mary as his wife (cf. Mt 1:16, 18-20, 24; Lk 1:27; 2:5).

> And while it is important for the Church to profess the virginal conception of Jesus, it is no less important to uphold Mary's marriage to Joseph, because juridically Joseph's fatherhood depends on it. Thus one understands why the generations are listed according to the genealogy of Joseph....
>
> St. Joseph was called by God to serve the person and mission of Jesus directly through the exercise of his fatherhood. It is precisely in this way that, as the Church's Liturgy teaches, he "cooperated in the fullness of time in the great mystery of salvation" and is truly a "minister of salvation."[21] His fatherhood is expressed concretely "in his having made his life a service, a sacrifice to the mystery of the Incarnation and to the redemptive mission connected with it; in having used the legal authority which was his over the Holy Family in order to make a total gift of self, of his life and work; in having turned his human vocation to domestic love into a superhuman oblation of self, an oblation of his heart and all his abilities into love placed at the service of the Messiah growing up in his house."[4]

About the mystery of Joseph's fatherhood, Lucien Deiss writes: "We can add that according to biblical tradition, fatherhood is always a call from God to welcome the child as a gift of God's love. Ever since the Covenant with Abraham, of which the external sign is circumcision, fertility has been the blessing par excellence which God grants to those who love God. More than any other fatherhood, Joseph's was a call from the God of the Covenant to welcome into his family this heaven-sent child. Is there a title to designate such fatherhood? Several have been proposed, all rather colorless.... Truly, there is no title on earth to designate such a fatherhood. The mystery of this fatherhood is akin to that of Mary's motherhood. Never in the history of humankind was there ever a virginal motherhood, a motherhood like Mary's. And never was there a fatherhood like Joseph's. When we say 'virginal motherhood,' we do not explain the mystery: we simply give it a name, the name befitting it according to the Scriptures.... When we speak of Joseph's fatherhood, neither do we explain the mystery: we simply give it a name, the name we read in the Scriptures. What gives this fatherhood its inexpressible beauty remains a secret between God and Joseph."[5]

Discrepancies in the Biblical Record?

Turning to the biblical record, we note that there are apparent discrepancies between the accounts of Jesus' birth and early life as reported in the Gospels of Matthew and Luke. Moreover the genealogies in each Gospel have a few key differences although it is obvious that both are structured differently (Matthew has 3 groups of 14 ancestors, Luke has 11 groups of 7 ancestors: in both cases we see multiples of 7 since it is the perfect number). We cannot simply explain away these "infancy narrative" variations. But such discrepancies underline the fact that the two Gospel narratives are independent accounts and not derivations of one from the other. This means too that the areas of agreement in their reports, such as the Virgin Birth, were truths taken for granted by all the early Christians. And the areas of agreement are substantial and far-reaching.

The genealogies of God-become-man are laid out in the opening of the Gospel of Matthew and the third chapter of the Gospel of Luke, in each case the structuring of the genealogies being customized to the writer's own particular perspective and objective. Those who stumble on the discrepancies in the two genealogies miss what is obvious and what is not immediately apparent. What is obvious is the fact that they are both artfully constructed to convey a message: for instance, Matthew's audience is Jewish and in wishing to show that Jesus is the Jewish messiah he begins with Abraham (and highlights David) while Luke is writing for Gentiles and begins with Adam to show that salvation is for both Jews and Gentiles.

Fr. Larry Toschi is candid about the difficulty posed by discrepancies in the genealogies:

> Despite the heroic attempts made throughout history to harmonize the genealogies of Matthew and Luke (Mt 1:1-17; Lk 3:23-38), no compelling argument has been found to show this is possible. A certain artificiality has been noted in each. In Matthew striking parallels found between Joseph of Nazareth and the patriarch Joseph make it small surprise that the fathers of both are named "Jacob" (Mt 1:16; Gen 35:22-24). In Luke strong resonances with 1 Samuel throughout the infancy narrative make the name of Joseph's father, "Heli," recall the priest who deals with Hannah and Samuel (Lk 3:23; 1 Sam 3:1). Be that as it may, it seems the differences must simply be accepted with the admission that either Matthew or Luke or both lacked sufficient accurate information to supply an authentic fully detailed genealogy, and that quite probably such detail was not essential to their purpose. Whether going back to Abraham or all the way to Adam and God, the two genealogies show absolute agreement in the central purpose of showing that Joseph,

a descendant of David, is the genealogical but not the biological father of Jesus, and conveys Davidic descent upon him.[6]

But what is not apparent on the surface is the fact that these are Jewish genealogies and therefore follow the "rules" of Jewish genealogies. "Son," "grandson" and even a grandson several times over will be called "son" because there is no other word for a descendant. "Son" also is used interchangeably between legal and biological sons and elaborate social rules require a man to sometimes become the "legal" father of a son who already has a biological father. It is to be assumed that all of these factors play a role in at least some of the apparent discrepancies in the genealogy. The key point to note is that the central players remain the same in both accounts: Abraham and David.

Perhaps the most startling of all the discrepancies is the name of Joseph's own father: Matthew says that Jacob is the father of Joseph while Luke says he is the son of Heli. One commentator observes that "actually we do not know the name of Saint Joseph's father. The gospels give us two genealogies for Jesus Christ. Saint Matthew writes (1:16): "Jacob begot Joseph, Mary's husband." Saint Luke writes (3:23): "Jesus, son (as it was thought) of Joseph, son of Heli." The two genealogies do not agree in some of the ancestral names given because neither genealogy aims to give a name for every generation. "Begot" and "son of" can span several generations. We do not know how many generations separated Saint Joseph from Heli and from Jacob."[7]

It has also been pointed out that the genealogies highlight four dimensions of Jesus' identity. He is Son of David (=king), Son of Abraham (=Jew), Son of Adam (=man) and Son of God (=God):

> "Though he does not center a good portion of his narrative on Davidic descent as Matthew does, Luke does clearly present the Son of God as the Davidic Messiah. Again it is through Joseph that Jesus is linked to David.... In Luke 1:27 the phrase "of the house of David" which grammatically follows Joseph's name refers to him alone, as is consistent with Luke 2:4 and 3:23. Joseph is introduced as important for introducing Mary. Before hearing the angel's words to her, the reader must know that she is a virgin betrothed to a man of the house of David. Joseph's role is what makes understandable the announcement that the Son of God conceived in Mary will be given "the throne of his father David, and he will reign over the house of Jacob for ever" (*Lk* 1:32-33).

The birth narrative similarly stresses that Joseph went for the census to Bethlehem, the city of David, "because he was of the house and lineage of David" (*Lk* 2:4). From their home in Nazareth, Mary journeys with him so that the child may be born in the city of David. Luke emphasizes Bethlehem more than Matthew, and the first announcement to the shepherds is that "in the city of David" is born a Savior, who is the Messiah, the Lord (*Lk* 2:11).

Luke's genealogy follows the infancy narrative and Jesus' baptism by John at the beginning of his ministry. John has told the people that being a descendant of Abraham is not sufficient for salvation, and that God's salvation is not limited by ancestry, for he can raise up children of Abraham from stones (*Lk* 3:8). At Jesus' baptism he is manifested as the beloved Son of heaven accompanied by the Holy Spirit (*Lk* 3:21-22). The genealogy sums up these two themes of human ancestry and divine Sonship by going back beyond Abraham, all the way to Adam and ultimately to God (*Lk* 3:38). Jesus initiates a course of history proceeding not only from Israel, but from humanity and from God Himself. Salvation is to be directed to all the children of Adam, equally created by God. Jesus' genealogy is traced through Joseph.

Jesus was "the son (as was supposed) of Joseph" (*Lk* 3:23). The "as was supposed" refers to the public being unaware of the virginal conception (*Lk* 1:27,34-37) and their considering Joseph to be the biological father, and to their not seeing beyond the human father to the divine Father of whom Jesus is Son in a more profound sense. Luke has portrayed Joseph as the transmitter of Davidic descent to Jesus quite apart from biological parenthood. Besides being the reputed father of Jesus, Joseph is the legal, genealogical father through whom Jesus traces his lineage.

Though the genealogy contains no markers, comments, or subdivisions, it has been shown to contain eleven groups of seven names, much as Matthew's three groups of fourteen could be broken into six groups of seven (the perfect number). Jesus has 77 ancestors listed, the last of whom is God. The names falling in the positions which are multiples of seven are significant, numbers 7 and 35 being two other Josephs. This list culminates with God whose number 77 is doubly perfect. It includes Abraham and David, the names given such importance by Matthew. It would seem that while using quite distinct forms, Matthew and Luke both emphasize Abraham, David, Joseph, and multiples of the number seven.

> While agreeing on Davidic descent, Luke differs from Matthew in showing this descent to occur through Nathan rather than Solomon. What is certain is that it is through Joseph that Jesus is son of David and son of Adam, the first human. The Son of God (*Lk* 1:35; 3:22,38) traces his human ancestry all the way back through creation by means of Joseph."[8]

With regard to the infancy narratives as a whole, Fr. Toschi has given a helpful overview of the discrepancies and the essential areas of agreement:

> While total harmonization is not possible and maybe not even too useful, there must be noted at least the possibility that the principle events related in the two Gospels could have all happened in the early years of Jesus' life. With minor changes of timing for moving from one place to another, for example, one can imagine a trip from Bethlehem to the Jerusalem temple and back, before the visit of the magi and the news of Herod's plot necessitates the escape into Egypt, while the later visit from Nazareth to the temple would have happened after Herod's death and the news of the birth of a rival king had been forgotten. The example of such a solution serves at least to caution one from over-emphasizing the inconsistencies in the two narratives.

Having recognized these difficulties relating to the scenes in which Joseph appears, it must then be admitted that there are no direct contradictions on anything essential to his identity. Joseph is present in the Gospels for what he contributes to the identity of Jesus. The reality of the incarnation required the Son of God to share the human condition also by having a human heritage and an upbringing by a human father. Independent of the historicity of certain of the episodes reported, the evangelists communicate the truth about Joseph's manner of fulfilling his role as father to the Messiah. With regard to this role, there is no contradiction but emphatic agreement.

The following are the conclusions that can safely be drawn about the person of Joseph from this study of the New Testament data. They are divided into three general categories.

BETROTHED AND HUSBAND TO MARY:

1. Joseph is betrothed to Mary when the conception occurs, but has had no sexual relations with her.
2. After the conception Joseph takes Mary into his home as wife.

3. Joseph and Mary share together their faith in the mystery and cooperate together to fulfill the mission of being parents to the Son of God.
4. As spouses Joseph and Mary show each other all the love and affection that results from their experience of God's love and that contributes providing a loving human family for Jesus.

Father of Jesus:

5. Because of the betrothal, Joseph is true, legal, genealogical father to Jesus, without being his biological father.
6. Joseph is of the line of David, and therefore passes on to Jesus the Davidic descent prophesied for the Messiah.
7. Joseph is in Bethlehem for the birth of Christ.
8. Joseph participates in naming the child "Jesus," "Savior."
9. Joseph exercises his role as father with affection, providing for his child, worrying about him, protecting and defending him, educating him in a profession and in the practice of obedience and religious observance.

10. Joseph is a carpenter, or worker in some other hard material.
11. Joseph lives in Nazareth of Galilee, and is therefore religiously, socially, and economically marginalized in the eyes of the Jerusalem authorities.
12. Joseph raises Jesus at Nazareth in a way that appears totally ordinary.
13. People know Jesus as Joseph's son.
14. Joseph never competes or interferes with Jesus' mission, but fades form the scene when the time comes to proclaim his divine Sonship, presumably having died by then.

MODEL OF FAITH-FILLED RESPONSE TO GOD:

15. Joseph is the last in the line of patriarchs who await fulfillment of the promise, and is especially prefigured by his Old Testament namesake.
16. Joseph is the recipient of divine communication and receives a special vocation to function as husband to Mary and father to Jesus.
17. Joseph is a man of exceptional faith, justice, and obedience.

18. Joseph is a model disciple, an anticipation of the Church.
19. With Mary, Joseph cooperates in the mystery of the incarnation in a unique way shared by no one else including the apostles.

The New Testament unquestionably presents the person of Joseph as the just and obedient son of David, chosen by God as husband to Mary and father to the Son of God and Messiah. He is father as a result of his betrothal and his response to the divine call. With Mary he is an unparalleled model of faith-filled collaboration with God's designs. He is an example of obedience to the God who in Jesus became subject to him.[9]

The Non-Historical Joseph

But before we go any further in our inquiry, we should set the record straight with respect to certain superstitions about Joseph that have sprung up over the centuries. These superstitions arose from the portrait of Joseph painted by the apocryphal writings that appeared after the second century. Although this portrait was never accepted or propagated by the Catholic Church it caused colossal damage because of its influence in the Eastern faith communities and among some of the Fathers.

The apocryphal works include: the Protoevangelium of James (second century); the Gospel of Thomas (third century); the Gospel of Pseudo-Matthew (fifth century); Coptic History of Joseph the Carpenter (sixth or seventh century); Gospel of the Nativity of Mary (sixth century or after); Arabic Gospel of the Infancy of the Savior (seventh century). None of these works derived from the Apostles although they often falsely used apostolic names to sell their product. It is not just that the authors had no link to the apostolic community. Just as important, they were written in eras so far removed in time from the events recounted in the Gospel as to lack any historical credibility. Consequently these works are just as unworthy of serious consideration as the so-called Gnostic gospels.

The earliest of the apocryphal works, the Protoevangelium of James, presents a fanciful portrait of Joseph based not on history but on its own theological agenda. It downplays the role of Joseph, denies that he is the father of Jesus, rejects the plain scriptural statement that he is married to Mary and arbitrarily affirms that he is an elderly man. All these apocryphal claims are not only wrong but demonstrably so. In fact the Gospels show the precise opposites of these claims to be true.

We see in Matthew and Luke that God entrusts Joseph with protecting and providing for Jesus and Mary. He was the head of the household. Again the Gospels portray Joseph as legally, spiritually and virginally the father of Jesus. They pointedly emphasize the fact that, through Joseph, Jesus is linked to Adam and to Israel. Joseph performs all the tasks and duties entrusted to fathers.

The elderly Joseph of the apocrypha is the most fanciful, and yet the most influential, of all the ideas in the Protoevangelium. It is easy to see that this arbitrary idea, invented to safeguard the truth of the virginity of Mary, is, at best, implausible. If he was an old man, how could he have endured the rigors of a journey from Israel to Egypt and back – protecting his family from brigands and the elements? How could he have supported the family with his physical labor if he was the one in need of support? Amusingly this invention is hardly helpful in "safeguarding" Mary's virginity. If Joseph was old, greater scandal would have resulted from the discovery that Mary is pregnant (since Joseph obviously would not be deemed capable of being the father).

The portrait of the apocryphal Joseph did not gain traction in the West thanks to St. Jerome who said:

> "Certain people who follow the ravings of the apocrypha fancy that the brethren of the Lord are sons of Joseph from another wife…We understand the brethren of the Lord NOT as sons of Joseph but the cousins of the Savior, children of Mary (the Lord's maternal aunt) who is said to be the mother of James the Less and Joseph and Jude…indeed, all Scripture indicates that cousins are called brethren."[10]

> "We can contend that Joseph had several wives because Abraham and Jacob had several wives, and that from these wives the brethren of the Lord were born – a fiction which most people invent with not so much pious as presumptuous audacity. You say that Mary did not remain a virgin; even more do I claim that Joseph also was virginal through Mary, in order that from a virginal marriage a virginal son might be born. For if the charge of fornication does not fall on this holy man, and if it is not written that he had another wife, and if he was more a protector than a husband of Mary, whom he was thought to have as his wife, it remains to assert that he who merited to be called the father of the Lord remained virginal with her."[11]

Jerome's argument was strongly supported by St. Thomas Aquinas who said: "We believe that just as the Mother of Jesus was a virgin, so was Joseph, because He placed the Virgin in the care of a virgin, and just as he did this at the close of his earthly life, so he did do it at the beginning [of his earthly life]. If the Lord was unwilling to commend His Virgin Mother to the care of anyone except a virgin, how could He have borne the fact that her husband had not been a virgin and remained as such."[12]

Suspicion or Awe?

In noting that the apocryphal works have no historical or theological value, we should also point out that they have influenced the interpretation of key biblical verses. Most important in this context is the passage about Joseph deciding to divorce Mary: "When his mother Mary was betrothed to Joseph, but before they lived together, she was found with child through the holy Spirit. Joseph her husband, since he was a righteous man, yet unwilling to expose her to shame, decided to divorce her quietly. Such was his intention when, behold, the angel of the Lord appeared to him in a dream and said, "Joseph, son of David, do not be afraid to take Mary your wife into your home. For it is through the holy Spirit that this child has been conceived in her." (Matthew 1:18-20). Do the texts tell us that Joseph's decision to divorce Mary was based on his suspecting her of adultery? Clearly not. But this is now the popular interpretation of this passage influenced in no small part by the apocrypha. But it is eminently reasonable to assume that Mary told Joseph that the child to be born of her is of God and that he, as a mere human being, did not think himself worthy of being espoused to the mother of the child. Hence his decision to separate – a decision he rescinds after receiving an angelic assurance. The very words of the angel to Joseph tell us that something more is afoot: "Do not be afraid to take Mary your wife into your home." Why "afraid"? The emotion more appropriate to adultery would be "anger." What "afraid" suggests is "awe." Fr. Toschi helps to show why the "suspicion" interpretation of the apocrypha is implausible:

"PROBLEMS WITH THE SUSPICION INTERPRETATION:

Since the time of the apocryphal *Protoevangelium of James*, many have interpreted this passage to say that Joseph suspected Mary of infidelity. Though Joseph is commonly the subject of active verbs in Matthew, verse 1:18 does not say that *he* found her with child. Instead one encounters the impersonal *heurethe* which is usually translated as passive voice "she was found," but which can also be middle voice: "she found herself" or simply "it happened that she was." Furthermore, the Greek does not so obviously separate the phrase "of the Holy Spirit" as our translations do, and as at least one translator wishes to emphasize by inserting a dash. The reading is *heurethe en gastri echousa ek pneumatos hagiou*, literally "found in the womb having of the Holy Spirit." The single discovery is conception by the Holy Spirit, the central point this passage is explaining. If one doubts whether Mary could have told Joseph of this mystery because Matthew seems unaware of any annunciation to Mary, one seems to be left with the less comprehensible situation of Mary herself not knowing the origin of her pregnancy. Mary would certainly have been aware of her virginity, and the lack of any human explanation for her condition. Matthew's silence on Mary's inner state is consistent with his purpose and approach in the infancy narrative developed around the person of Joseph, but this does not eliminate the need for some kind of divine communication to Mary, at least in the interior of her heart, and an invitation to a faith response on her part. If Mary did not tell Joseph, she would not only be insensitive and mistrusting, but even unfair to the natural rights of her betrothed husband. Of course, one might easily conjecture that Joseph did not believe her, since it is difficult to imagine having that much faith. Yet it is precisely this extraordinary faith that Matthew describes to his readers: Joseph is the just man who consistently believes and acts upon God's messages relating to the Messiah.

In response to this suspicion theory, then, the whole passage must be examined, particularly the meaning of "just man" and of "do not fear." It must be noted, though, that Matthew makes no mention of any suspicion on the part of Joseph. An unprejudiced reading of Matthew 1:18 leads one to understand that Mary and Joseph and perhaps others in their families knew of Mary's pregnancy and of its divine origin. There is no need to suppose that "of the Holy Spirit" is added for the reader's knowledge, while unknown to Joseph. Such an interpretation leads to the conclusion that the phrase is an unusual, superfluous, redactional addition, instead of allowing it to be taken at face value.

JOSEPH'S JUSTICE:

A very large body of literature, both ancient and contemporary, exists to explain the meaning of "just man" and its relationship to Joseph, who "unwilling to put her to shame, resolved to divorce her quietly" (Mt 1:19). The hypothesis of Joseph's suspicion has occasioned many difficulties in the resulting attempts to interpret his justice in terms of his reaction to the law in the face of this suspicion.

Pg. 33-34
The Angel's Message:

The passage contains many standard elements of annunciations of births and commissioning. One of these elements is evidenced in the Lord's messenger addressing him by name and by the title that signifies the important role he is to play, "Joseph, son of David" (Mt 1:20), much as Gideon is addressed as "you mighty man of valor" (Jgs 6:12). The words that follow, "do not fear," are certainly a common formula uttered by angels in the New Testament (Mt 28:5,10; Lk 1:13, 30; 5:10; Acts 18:9), but are by no means trivial. They refer precisely to the awe that Joseph is experiencing at the virginal conception and now at the appearance of the angel while he is in the midst of planning the difficult separation from Mary. Here another parallel can be seen in Judges 6: Gideon fears because he has "seen the angel of the Lord face to face," whom no one can see and still live (Ex 33:20), and he must be reassured "do not fear, you shall not die" (Jgs 6:22-23). The angel's "do not fear" is not spoken to Joseph simply to relieve whatever feelings might accompany suspicion. Such feelings would perhaps be more like hurt, sorrow, anger, or jealousy, but not "fear" in the sense of *phobeomai*. Like Tobias (Tob 6:15-17), Joseph needs a communication from God to know that he is divinely chosen for this marriage.

Current translations of Matthew 1:20 are based on the suspicion hypothesis and separate "do not fear to take Mary your wife" from what follows by a comma, and by a conjunction such as "for," thus interpreting that the clause "that which is conceived in her is of the Holy Spirit" is new information for Joseph. Such news, however, would hardly be a reason to allay fear in the above biblical sense, but rather a cause for it. Grammatical analysis of the conjunctions *gar* and *de* in Matthew 1:20 shows that they may be interpreted in the sense of "indeed… but," rather than "for…and." The angel is telling Joseph that he should not hesitate to continue with the marriage, for though Mary is indeed pregnant by the Holy Spirit, he is nevertheless to have an important role in that work: to act as Mary's husband and to name the child."[13]

Did Joseph and Mary Have Other Children?

Inevitably, any study of Joseph, Mary and Jesus, leads to the question of the "brothers and sisters" of Jesus mentioned in the Bible. The perpetual virginity of Mary is denied by many of today's Christians. Eastern and Oriental Orthodox Christians affirm the virginity of Mary but not of Joseph. This is because they rely on the apocryphal gospels that depict Joseph as an old widower with children from a previous marriage. We have seen why these apocrypha are not historical. Here we will see why Christians from the early first millennium have always affirmed the perpetual virginity of Mary.

The discovery of the human Jesus, the New Adam, is inescapably a discovery of Mary, the New Eve. Although systematically articulated over centuries, the fundamental insight was in place at the start of the Christian era. The insight encompassed essential corollaries: immaculate conception, divine maternity, perpetual virginity, assumption, mediation/intercession.

Two of these corollaries, in particular, have been rejected in recent years by various Protestant Christians: the continued virginity of Mary and Marian intercession/mediation. But neither truth can be negotiated away or ignored without denaturing Christian doctrine as a whole.

We will now address the question of what is usually called the perpetual virginity of Mary. Here the issues are fairly clearcut: the Gospels pointedly refer to the brothers and sisters of Jesus and certain passages in the Gospels seem to imply that Joseph and Mary had other children after Jesus.

In the normal course of things, when reading a text we should adopt the simplest and most obvious interpretation of its content. The burden of proof is on anyone who wishes to argue to the contrary. But when two sets of texts in the same work say something seemingly contradictory, then it behooves us to take a more nuanced approach. The burden of proof, in fact, is on those who ignore the conflict and defiantly insist on sticking with their preferred version.

Certainly the Gospels speak of James, Joses/Joseph, Simon, and Judas as brothers of Jesus. But the very same Gospels say that James/Joses are sons of "the other" Mary, not the sons of Mary, the Mother of Jesus. In Matthew 13 we read of James and Joseph, the brothers of Jesus. In Matthew 27 we read that this James and Joseph are the sons of "the other Mary". In Mark 6 we read of James and Joses, the brothers of Jesus. In Mark 15-16, the same James and Joses are seen to be the sons of another Mary.

There are other factors that should give us clues to the subtleties at play: nowhere in the Gospels are we told that Joseph or Mary had any children other than Jesus; Jesus is called the Son of Mary or the Son of Joseph suggesting that he was the only son; on the Cross, Jesus hands his Mother to the care of John, an unthinkable act if he had siblings; finally, we know that the Greek words for brother and sister were also used to refer to kinfolk and in fact in certain Eastern cultures cousins are still called "brothers" and "sisters."

What about Judas and Simon, the other "brothers," and the "sisters" of Jesus? The Bible does not have much to say on this beyond the cryptic opening of the epistle of Jude: "Jude, a slave of Jesus Christ and brother of James." (Jude 1:1). We shall see, however, what the earliest historians of the Church had to say about the matter. But before that we should note that, in Matthew 27 and Mark 15, James and Joses/Joseph are mentioned before Simon and Judas. We know that the first two were not Jesus' blood brothers and it seems most unlikely that Simon and Judas would be mentioned after them if they were indeed blood brothers. The same goes for the "sisters."

The theologian François Rossier considers the issue of terminology :

> There are no "cousins" in the New Testament, except for one case. We find the word *anepsios* once, in Colossians 4:10. Most scholars today think that the Letter to the Colossians was not written by Paul, but probably by a disciple of his from the second generation of Christians with a Greek background. Otherwise, we find the word *adelphos* 343 times in the New Testament (and *adelphê*, "sister," 26 times), but no other "cousin." The only family relationship that existed among people of a same generation in the New Testament seems to be brotherhood. Is it relevant, since we know that in Judaic society the inmost family group was not limited to the nuclear family as we know it in North America or in Europe? Other Greek words such as *homopatôr* ("half-brother by the father") or *homomêtôr* ("half-brother by the mother") are also not found in the New Testament. If the authors of the New Testament wanted to render the relationships within Jesus' family as precisely as possible in Greek, they should have used such expressions since--and Matthew and Luke make it very clear--Jesus was not the true son of Joseph. If Jesus' "brothers" were sons of Mary, they would have been only Jesus' "half-

brothers by the mother," and there was a Greek word for that….

Nowhere in the New Testament are the "brothers" of Jesus also identified as "sons of Mary" within the same context. Whereas, again in Mark 6:3, Jesus is identified as "the son of Mary" by the people of Nazareth….

The vast majority of the Fathers of the Church, supporting either the Epiphanian or the Jeromian hypothesis, belonged to the Greek culture and spoke Greek. Some of them were even close to the New Testament era in both time and culture. Yet they did not find it an obstacle to consider Jesus' *adelphoi* as his cousins, step-brothers or half-brothers. The tradition adopted that point of view-- be it the Catholic one, the Orthodox one, or even the Reformation one (with Luther and Calvin)--until the nineteenth century, when Protestant biblical scholars started to question the consensus in the name of the historical-critical method of interpretation. Their views were widely adopted within the Protestant denominations, making of Mary's perpetual virginity one of the great markers of dissent.[14]

One interesting barrier in shedding any further light is the bewildering array of Jameses and Marys in the New Testament.

Lets start with the Jameses. There is James the Greater, son of Zebedee and the brother of the Apostle John. Then there is James the Lesser, the Son of Alphaeus. Then we have James the brother of Joseph/Joses who is the son of "the other Mary." Finally we have James the brother of the Lord, bishop of Jerusalem, who is also called an Apostle. We could add to the mix James the brother of the author of the epistle of Jude.

With regard to the Marys, we have Mary the mother of Jesus, Mary Magdalene, Mary the mother of James and Joses and Mary of Clopas. "Standing by the cross of Jesus were his mother, and his mother's sister, Mary the wife of Clopas, and Mary Magdalene" (*John* 19:25).

So who's who here? One possible approach is this. James the Lesser is described in the Gospels as "James, the son of Alphaeus." (Matthew 10:3). "Clopas," it has been pointed out, is the Greek form of the Aramaic name "Alphaeus." Mary of Clopas is then the mother of James and Joseph/Joses and the James in question here is also the Apostle James the Lesser. Clopas, according to the earliest Church historians, was the brother of Joseph and therefore his sons would be cousins of Jesus – or "brothers" in Aramaic usage. Thus James is called one of the brothers of Jesus in the Gospels and then "the brother of the Lord" in the Acts of the Apostles and in Galatians. One item from early tradition is relevant here. It has been held that after the death of Joseph, Jesus and Mary lived with the family of Clopas (possibly in Capernaum). This would make Clopas' children foster-brothers and sisters of Jesus – and hence the reference to them as brothers and sisters of Jesus was more natural even than "cousins".

The life of James the Just, bishop of Jerusalem, has been recorded both by the Jewish historian Josephus and the second-century Christian writer Hegesippus. Hegesippus also sheds light on Simon/Simeon, the brother of the Lord mentioned in the Gospels: "After James the Just was martyred, on the same charge as the Lord, then Simeon being also his [Jesus'] uncle's child, the son of Clopas, was appointed as bishop, as second in succession, being put forward by all, being the cousin of the Lord."[15] Hegesippus pointedly says about Judas that he was "called his [the Lord's] brother"[16]; here "called" implies that he was not actually a blood brother. Thus there is good reason to believe that James, Joseph, Simon, Judas and their sisters were children of Clopas and Mary.

Two objections to Mary's perpetual virginity hinge on certain verses. "He [Joseph] had no relations with her until she bore a son, and he named him Jesus." (Matthew 1:25). Does this mean, as the critics say, that Joseph had sexual relations after Jesus was born? No, it is a negative statement that he was not involved in the conception of Jesus not a positive statement that he had relations after the birth of Jesus. In his notes to the Geneva Bible (1560), John Calvin points out that "Neither yet doest this worde (til) import always a time following: wherein the contrarie may be affirmed, as our Saviour, saying that he wil be present with his disciples, til the end of the world meaneth not, that after this worlde he wil not be with them." A manual of Methodist doctrine said about this verse: "It cannot be inferred from that expression, 'Michal had no child till the day of her death' (2 Sam 6:23) that she had children afterward."[17]

Another line of attack centers on Luke 2:7: "And she gave birth to her firstborn son." Here it should be noted that according to the Jews the child that opened the womb is the first-born (Exodus 13:2; Numbers 3:12). There is no implication that the child is the first of many. An ancient tomb inscription states that the mother died as she was giving birth to her first-born. As John Calvin put it, "first-born" refers to the fact "she had never none before, and not in respect of any she had after."

Now all of this should be taken in conjunction with the decisive issue: the question of how you determine which interpretation is to serve us authoritative. It takes no great research to see that not just the leaders of the "early Church" but even the Protestant Reformers were unanimous in affirming the perpetual virginity of Mary as a truth of faith. They all had the same texts that we have today and yet they saw no contradiction in affirming Jesus as the only Son of his mother. Of course, the earliest members of the Church were contemporaries of the "brothers" of Jesus and it was a linguistic and cultural fact of their era that "brothers" and "sisters" referred to kinfolk not just blood siblings. The proliferation of the apocrypha in the second century and after shows that the faithful were concerned not simply with affirming the Virgin Birth but also the perpetual virginity. Only in the fourth century was there any serious deviation from this teaching but this ended (like other instances of deviation from Christian doctrine) after decisive refutations first from the Fathers and then from a Church Council.

Authoritative Interpretation

In discussing biblical texts, the issue of authoritative interpretation is decisive. Every doctrine is an interpretation. Now the Bible is not simply a novel concerning which different literary critics can foist their own creative spins. Christians consider it to be an account of God's revelation to humanity. Nevertheless, it is a revelation laid out in specific written narratives and letters. How should these narratives and letters be understood? Where are the boundaries between "historical episode" and "theological teaching"? What about the nuances of translation? When there is an obvious theological statement ("Faith without works is dead") how is it to be understood?

Now there are two basic approaches to this problem: either there is one authoritative interpretation of the divine Word that holds true from the inception of the Church to the present day or every believer determines the interpretation of all biblical passages on his or her own. The first position is that held by the Catholic Church and the second, of course, is the Protestant position. But even Protestants, for the most part, hold that there are certain interpretations of biblical passages that are normative and binding for all believers, i.e., authoritative. So much so, even if one or more biblical passages appear to contradict an authoritative interpretation, the burden of proof is in favor of the interpretation. When Jesus says, "The Father is greater than I" (John 14:28), this statement should not be seen as contradicting the doctrine that the Three Persons of the Trinity are co-equal. For that matter the doctrine of the Trinity is not spelled out as such in Scripture and its formulation took place over centuries despite the problem of certain seemingly inconsistent texts. In fact, every Christian group, if it wishes to be recognized as such, maintains a Trinitarian interpretation of Scripture. To be sure, various sects have broken off from Christianity appealing in many cases to biblical passages that seem inconsistent with the doctrine of the Trinity. Nevertheless, the majority of Protestant denominations hold to this doctrine thus implicitly acknowledging the role of authoritative interpretations.

How does someone with a Protestant frame of reference determine that an interpretation is authoritative? The argument about the inner testimony of the Holy Spirit is insufficient because there are Protestants who disagree among themselves on key doctrines (soteriology, ecclesiology, eschatology) and in such cases each claimant appeals to this inner testimony. And those authoritative interpretations that we have today did not simply spring out of some individual's claim to testimony from the Holy Spirit. In point of fact these authoritative interpretations have two sources: the witness of the Church Fathers and the teaching of the first seven Ecumenical Councils. In practice, Protestants like Catholics and Orthodox take the interpretations of the Councils to be definitive. Protestants may not put as much stock in the Fathers but they do accept the dogmatic definitions of the Councils.

Now sometimes Protestants say they accept the Councils because the conciliar teachings conform with Scripture. But it can then be asked how they know that the Councils' teachings conform with Scripture. If they say that in their personal opinion the Councils are faithful to Scripture then the ultimate arbiter is personal opinion. But if the Trinity has no greater basis for its truth than personal opinion then you cannot fault someone whose personal opinion leads them to reject the doctrine as "unbiblical". Pushed into this corner, most of them concede that the Councils do have some level of authority in determining the interpretation of Scripture when it comes to key doctrines. The few who have no role for the Councils end up in one of two places: either they leave Christianity as a whole because no one can really decide what's Christian doctrine or (inconsistently) they stick to the teachings of the Councils while saying the Councils have no authority. As a whole, however, Protestants accept the teachings of the Council.

Now it so happens that three of the Seven Ecumenical Councils of the undivided Church affirmed Mary's perpetual virginity in the clearest terms. Thus the Second Council of Constantinople (553) spoke of "the holy, glorious, ever-Virgin Mary." The Third Council of Constantinople (680) accepted and ratified the teaching of the First Lateran Council (649) which decreed, "If anyone does not in accord with the Holy Fathers acknowledge the holy and ever virgin and immaculate Mary was really and truly the Mother of God, inasmuch as she, in the fullness of time, and without seed, conceived by the Holy Spirit, God in the Word Himself, who before all time was born of God the Father, and without loss of integrity brought Him forth, and after His birth preserved her virginity inviolate, let him be condemned." Finally, the Seventh Ecumenical Council (the Second Council of Nicaea, 787) proclaims, "If any one does not confess that the holy, **ever virgin Mary**, really and truly the Mother of God, is higher than all creatures visible and invisible, and does not implore with a sincere faith, her intercession, given her powerful access to our God born of her, let him be anathema."

Faced with this clear teaching, Catholics, Orthodox and Protestants up to the 19th century accepted the perpetual virginity of Mary as a truth of faith and a binding interpretation of the scriptural texts.

Today, many Protestants deny the doctrine without realizing its roots in the Councils of the Church. But if they deny one dogma defined by one of these Seven Ecumenical Councils, then in terms of their own frame of reference, they cannot consistently affirm any of the other dogmas as authoritative. The dogmas of Christ's two natures and of the Three Persons in one Godhead are accepted as final interpretations because the Councils defined them. If you do accept these as definitive, you can't consistently say that the Council was authoritative in some interpretations but not in others (how could you know which is authoritative and which isn't). You can't have your cake and eat it too. It's all or nothing. The doctrine of Mary's perpetual virginity is a defined dogma of the Seven Ecumenical Councils along with other foundational doctrines of Christianity. If you reject the Councils' authority when it comes to this doctrine then you can't consistently defend any of its other doctrines as authoritative. So a denial of Mary's perpetual virginity strikes at the very root of orthodox Christianity.

Also under the category of interpretation is the witness of the Fathers of the Church. These are the great and ancient interpreters of Scripture whose interpretations have been taken as normative by generations of Christians, Protestant, Catholic and Orthodox. Any doctrine taught unanimously by the Fathers of East and West is generally considered authoritative by that very fact. These are the same holy thinkers whose teachings and interpretations helped guide the Councils to their conclusions. Now it is a striking fact that no Father of the Church, East or West, has denied the perpetual virginity of Mary. Several have written their own striking expositions of the doctrine. Jose Pedrozo notes that Fathers with different styles and agendas taught the doctrine: Athanasius of Alexandria, Ephraem of Syria, Hilary of Poitiers, John Chrysostom, Ambrose of Milan, and Augustine of Hippo. Of one Father, Tertullian, it has been said that he seemed to be in doubt about the doctrine – but Pedrozo has shown that Tertullian's comments were ambiguous at best.[18] Now the Fathers were closer in time to the apostolic era. They were closer to the writers of Scripture and their intentions and to the beliefs of the first Christians than anyone today. And yet these great witnesses speak with one voice about the fact that Mary was always virgin. Why should we discount their interpretations? And this is precisely why no Christian seriously questioned the doctrine for 19 centuries (with one solitary exception: Helvidius, Jovinian and Bonosus dissented from the doctrine in the last two decades of the fourth century but this dissent died a quick death after it was roundly condemned by the Fathers).

The consensus on the matter did not change with the Protestant Reformation. Martin Luther said, "It is an article of faith that Mary is Mother of the Lord and still a virgin. ... Christ, we believe, came forth from a womb left perfectly intact."[19] Calvin who said that God granted Mary the "highest honor" by choosing and destining her to be "the Mother of his Son" said "Helvidius has shown himself too ignorant, in saying that Mary had several sons, because mention is made in some passages of the brothers of Christ."[20] Ulrich Zwingli said, "I firmly believe that Mary, according to the words of the gospel as a pure Virgin brought forth for us the Son of God and in childbirth and after childbirth forever remained a pure, intact Virgin."[21]

Now it seems unthinkable – and therefore unbelievable – that a doctrine held as definitive Christian truth by all Christians for nearly 2000 years can be rejected as false simply because a few Christians starting in the 19th century decided that all previous generations of Christians were wrong.

After all, no new facts have turned up, no new textual passages have been discovered. What has happened is simply that certain iconoclasts have decided that they will cut themselves free of their roots and strike out on their own. Why should we trust these iconoclasts whose own interpretations are subjective, arbitrary and liable to change in a generation or less?

Incidentally, those Christians who retain belief in the Virgin Birth while denying Mary's perpetual virginity will eventually end up losing belief in both. This was the prescient warning issued by the Reformer Ulrich Zwingli: "It was not enough that the conception of Jesus take place without a male role, for if a woman who had previously known a man had conceived him even through the Holy Spirit, 'who would ever have believed that the child that was born was of the Holy Spirit? For nature knows no birth that is not besmirched with stain.' For the same reason she had to be ever a virgin, she who bore the one in whom there could not be even the least suspicion of blemish. For the birth of Jesus to be absolutely pure of every stain, Mary herself had to be free of any pollution of normal child-bearing."[22] Historically this was what happened. The Enlightenment rejection of the doctrine of perpetual virginity accompanied the denial not simply of the Virgin Birth but of the divinity of Christ.

Also relevant here is the liturgy. Perhaps the truest witness to the faith of the believing community is the language of their prayer and liturgical celebration. All of the ancient liturgies, even those before the Council of Ephesus, testify to the firm belief of the Christian faithful in the veneration of the "ever-Virgin". The Eastern liturgies, the most ancient of them all since Christianity sprang in the East, resonate with hymns, odes and prayers to the Ever-Virgin Mary. The Byzantine liturgy for instance proclaims, "O Christ, behold Thy Mother, she who conceived Thee in her womb, without the loss of her virginity, and who after she had given Thee birth remained a stainless Virgin." The Ethiopian liturgy declares, "O holy praiseful ever-virgin Parent of God, Mother of Christ." These are the great prayers that formed the Christian soul, the database that transmits to this very day the living faith of the Apostles. The decline of a full-blooded faith in modern times can be traced at least partially to the loss of the ancient liturgy in its fullness. Christians who do not live the liturgy of their fathers in faith are like fish out of water and so cannot hope to recognize the true teachings of ancient Christianity. The loss of the liturgy results first in the loss of a living faith and the sense of the sacred and second in the loss of the doctrines that constitute Christianity.

Of course, it was not just the virginity of Mary that was seen as relevant but also that of Joseph. Jerome was the great defender of a truth that was recognized as fundamental: the perpetual virginity of both Joseph and Mary. Said Jerome: "Joseph himself was a virgin through Mary, so that a virgin son might be born of a virgin wedlock." "He who was deemed worthy to be called the father of the Lord remained a virgin, with Mary." (18).

Now that we have addressed the question of the virginity of Joseph and Mary, we will take up one other unfortunately widespread misconception relevant to our discussion: the historicity of the narratives pertaining to the early life of Jesus.

Are the "Infancy" Narratives Historical Facts or Legendary After-thoughts?

How do we know that the so-called infancy narratives, namely the accounts of the angelic annunciations and early life of Jesus in the Gospels of Matthew and Luke, are historically accurate? This question is raised because certain fashionable methodologies in New Testament scholarship of the late nineteenth century and first half of the twentieth century produced eccentric but highly influential ways of reading the Gospels. No new historical facts were uncovered. Rather theories were proposed as to the origins of the source material for the Gospels, the literary structures used in presenting this material, the chronological sequence of the appearance of the material. Much of this thinking was pure speculation with assumptions and conclusions that were incapable of historical confirmation. What traditions lie behind a particular text, which sayings of Jesus are authentic, which pre-Gospel literary sources lie behind the Gospel narratives, which parts of the Gospels may be taken simply as mythological or metaphorical, which Gospel came first and is thereby (so it was claimed) more historically accurate? Inevitably, the answers to these questions were subjective, arbitrary, mutually incompatible and cursed by short product expiration dates; they rested entirely on speculation (albeit voluminous speculation). But fashions come and go. The good news is that there is a return to sanity in large pockets of mainstream New Testament studies. By sanity we refer to the willingness to study the evidence as it stands rather than viewing it with pet peeves or theories.

Many scholars have re-discovered what was known to the pre-modern masses: Jesus was Jewish and his actions and sayings must be understood with that in mind rather than through the ideological prism of a German, British or even American theologian.

Just as significant, it is now recognized that the Gospels are, believe it or not, biographies. Now this seemed to be a glimpse of the obvious to the unlearned of the first 1800 years of Christian history but, for the last several decades, it was believed that they were just collections of traditions or sayings and should be treated as such.

With the publication of Charles Talbert's *What is a Gospel?* (1977) and Richard Burridge's *What Are the Gospels? A Comparison with Greco-Roman Biography* (1992), however, there has been a dramatic turnabout in moden scholarship. It is today widely recognized that the older theories were mistaken and the Gospels belong to a biographical genre common in the Greco-Roman world. "Very few books on the Gospels have influenced scholarly opinion more strongly," wrote Cambridge New Testament scholar Graham Stanton in his introduction to the second edition of Burridge's book. "I do not think it is now possible to deny that the Gospels are a sub-set of the broad ancient literary genre of 'lives,' that is, biographies."[24] We realize now that in the Gospels we are dealing with what were seen as standard biographies of Jesus that were intended to convey historical fact rather than quilts of sayings and traditions.

As for the chronological sequence of the composition of the Gospels, the German hypothesis (introduced first in 1863) that Mark came first is no longer taken for granted. A significant minority of New Testament scholars holds that textual and other evidence point to the priority of the Gospel of Matthew. Moreover, even key defenders of Markan priority today admit that the current version of Mark was clearly written after Matthew. They rest their case on a proto-Mark now lost! (This was, for instance, the position taken by Harvard New Testament scholar Helmut Koester, a student of Rudolf Bultmann and president of the Society of Biblical Literature who wrote the "standard reference work" introducing the New Testament).

There are also hypotheses of documents that were supposedly prepared before any of the current Gospels. But speculations are hardly a solid basis for a theory offered as as "Gospel truth"! The encyclopedic 2011 book *New Studies in the Synoptic Problem* carries the proceedings of the Oxford Conference of the Synoptic Problem attended by leading scholars representing different views of the sequence of the Gospels. Significantly, in his contribution to the volume, Christopher Tuckett, in whose honor the conference was held, concluded that: "We are (hopefully) all now much more aware of the provisional nature of any alleged "solutions" to the Synoptic Problem, and aware too that between our (sometimes neat and simple) solutions and historical reality may lie an unbridgeable chasm."[25]

In *The Gospel of Jesus*, William Farmer argues that Markan priority was largely driven by a Prussian attempt to subvert the Matthean basis for the papacy: "This helps to explain how a critical mass of scholarly opinion, despite convincing evidence to the contrary, formed in favor of Markan primacy, so that during the first half of the twentieth century it became possible for almost all scholars to believe (what today almost all scholars have come to disbelieve) that the Two-Source Hypothesis was an 'assured result' of nineteenth-century German scholarship."[26]

With regard to chronological sequence, Clement of Alexandria (cited by Eusebius) points to a tradition "on the order of the Gospels" handed down by "the elders who lived in the first days." According to these elders, the two Gospels with genealogies (Matthew and Luke) were written first, followed by Mark and John; later commentators said that Mark did not include a birth narrative because it was already found in the earlier Gospels. All the early Church Fathers who wrote about this matter held to Matthew as the first Gospel.

Farmer notes that "Eusebius the great historian of the early church, preserves for us information going back to the primitive elders of the church in the first quarter of the second century. Eusebius informs us that the Gospels with genealogies (certainly including Matthew and Luke) were composed before those without genealogies.... It is very important to emphasize that nothing in church history supports the idea of Markan priority."[27]

So what does all this have to do with the historicity of the infancy narratives? Plenty. First, consider the nature of Greco-Roman biographies. Burridge points out that Greco-Roman biographies center on the ancestry, birth, education, character traits, deeds, death and influence of its subjects. He writes, "If we compare the synoptic gospels with our bioi, we note that Matthew goes straight into the subject's ancestry, like Nepos and Plutarch; Mark, however, like Xenophon, begins with just one sentence, while some of Plutarch's Lives start straight in (e.g. Timoleon 1). Luke's use of a preface can be paralleled in Lucian and Philo, who have a paragraph each, and in Isocrates, Tacitus and Philostratus, who all have a more extended prologue. Thus the various beginnings of the synoptic gospels reflect the range of possibilities for bioi with respect to an opening sentence or preface. Also, like most Graeco-Roman bioi, Mark and Matthew include the name of their subject at the very start."

The fact that comparatively little is said about Jesus' early life in the Gospels is different from modern but not Greco-Roman biographies. "The allocation of space within the gospels is one reason often cited against them being biographies. It is pointed out that we are told little or nothing of the first thirty or so years of Jesus' life, and then there is the large concentration of space devoted to his death. In fact, our analysis of bioi revealed that the first thirty or forty years of a subject's life can be dealt with very briefly, or even omitted, while the death-scene is usually exaggerated. Matthew and Luke devote just over 15% of their text to the events of the Last Supper, Trial, Passion and Resurrection, while Mark has rather more, 19.1%. If these figures are compared with those given to their subject's last days and death by Plutarch (17.3%), Nepos (15%), Tacitus (10%) and Philostratus (26%), then the gospels' allocation of space does not look out of place or puzzling."[28]

In brief, given that Greco-Roman biographies include sections on the ancestry and birth of the protagonist, the infancy narratives in Matthew and Luke make sense. But there are other issues. Some of the older critics charged that the infancy narratives were later creations tacked on to the Gospel collections of traditions and sayings. But any study of Matthew and Luke indicate that such later addition is improbable for various reasons.

First, the entire unity of both Gospels depends on the infancy narratives since the themes in these narratives are further developed in the rest of each of these Gospels.

> "The thematic and theological unity of Luke 1-2 with the rest of Luke's Gospel has been demonstrated (Minear). Various of Luke's major themes are given their first airing in the birth narratives."[29]

> "The 20 Lucan themes investigated by J. Navone (Themes of St. Luke [Rome, 1970]) are already enunciated in 1:5-2:52: banquet, conversion, faith, fatherhood, grace, Jerusalem, joy, kingship, mercy, poverty, prayer, prophet, salvation, spirit, temptation, today, universalism, way, witness."[30]

> "It testifies to Matthew's art that the infancy narratives, like an operatic overture, touches on themes that characterize his gospel: a full revelation of Jesus' divine identity, and the responses of acceptance and rejection that it evoked. Theologically, it is one scriptural

authority for the later doctrine of the incarnation."[31]

Secondly, the earliest non-scriptural writings of Christians show that the infancy narratives were considered an integral part of the story of Jesus. For instance, Ignatius of Antioch writing in his Letter to the Smyrnaeans in 110 AD affirms that Jesus "was truly of the seed of David according to the flesh, and the Son of God according to the will and power of God; that He was truly born of a virgin" – affirmations that include Joseph and Mary. Other early Christian writers like Justin Martyr and Irenaeus refer likewise to the infancy narratives. Moreover, none of the first critics of Christianity suggested that the infancy narratives were later additions.

Yet other critiques claim that the infancy narratives were created out of pagan myth or Old Testament prophecies. But both charges are thoroughly implausible. There is nothing remotely similar to these narratives in any pagan myth. According to one historian, "if one puts all the schemas that have been proposed together and looks for common elements, the results that emerge are often vague or unhelpful. For instance, the hero will typically have a miraculous conception or birth – but it is hardly legitimate to compare the story of the virgin birth recounted in the Gospels with, say, Zeus raping Leda in the form of a swan simply because both involve some sort of supernatural element."[32]

Craig Keener writes: "Ancient biographers sometimes praised the miraculous births of their subjects (especially prominent in the Old Testament), but there are no close parallels to the virgin birth. Greeks told stories of gods impregnating women, but the text indicates that Mary's conception was not sexual; nor does the Old Testament (or Jewish tradition) ascribe sexual characteristics to God. Many miraculous birth stories in the ancient world (including Jewish accounts, e.g., 1 Enoch 106) are heavily embroidered with mythical imagery (e.g., babies filling houses with light), in contrast with the straightforward narrative style of this passage (cf. similarly Ex 2:1–10)."[33]

Other New Testament scholars note:

"In our discussion of the genre of the birth Narratives we noted that any comparison of Matthew 1–2 and Luke 1–2 to pagan divine birth stories leads to the conclusion that the Gospel stories cannot be explained simply on the basis of such comparisons. This is particularly the case in regard to the matter of the virginal conception, for what we find in Matthew and Luke is not the story of some sort of sacred marriage (hieros gamos) or a divine being descending to earth and, in the guise of a man, mating with a human woman, but rather the story of a miraculous conception without aid of any man, divine or other wise. The Gospel story is rather about how Mary conceived without any form of intercourse through the agency of the Holy Spirit. As such this story is without precedent either in Jewish or pagan literature, even including the OT."[34]

As for the idea that the infancy narratives are simply a creation out of Old Testament prophecies, Craig Keener notes, "Some scholars suggest that Matthew interprets Jesus in light of the Old Testament and that he therefore does not stick very close to the story of Jesus. But while it is true that Matthew interprets Jesus in light of the Old Testament, he also interprets the Old Testament record in light of Jesus. If Matthew simply invented stories about Jesus' infancy to fit Old Testament messianic texts, he should have chosen more obvious texts to start with and created stories that matched them better. Like most Greek-speaking Jewish biographers, Matthew is more interested in interpreting tradition than in creating it."[35]

If anything, the actual train of events left the Evangelists struggling to find Old Testament passages that might explain them. About Jeremiah 31:15 and Hosea 11:1, R.T. France comments that neither "was interpreted Messianically at the time; and the 'quotation' in Matthew 2:23 does not appear in the Old Testament at all...In fact the aim of the formula-quotations in chapter 2 seems to be primarily apologetic, explaining some of the unexpected features in Jesus' background, particularly his geographical origins. It would be a strange apologetic which invented 'facts' in order to defend them!"[36]

Why is there no infancy narrative in Mark or John? This is a problem only for those who hold fast to Markan priority. As early Christian thinkers have pointed out, if the infancy narratives had already been laid out in Matthew and Luke, neither Mark nor John have any reason to recapitulate what has already been narrated. For that matter, Luke does not need to say what Matthew has already covered – another possible explanation for their diverging accounts. The Gospels were not intended to be carbon copies of each other. Not only was each written for a different audience (and accordingly modulated) but for the most part they reflect the author's perspective on the same foundational events and his access to additional data-points.

Postscript – the Two Josephs

One of the enduring mysteries in Scripture is the parallelism of the Old Testament and New Testament Josephs. These are parallels that could not have been invented or contrived given the sheer improbability of the unique life trajectory of each of the Josephs.

Here are the obvious parallels:

- They are both named Joseph.
- They both have fathers named Jacob.
- They both "go down" to Egypt because of hostile forces.
- They are both "just," obedient and pure.
- They are both "dreamers" who receive supernatural instructions through their dreams.
- They are both rulers of the house of their king: the Pharaoh in the case of the first Joseph and the Son of God in the case of the second.
- They are both vehicles providing bread to the world: physical bread in the case of the first Joseph and the Bread from Heaven in the second.

- About the first Joseph, it was said "Go to Joseph" if you are in need. How much truer is this the case with the second Joseph.

The Testimony of "Tradition"

As with our study of the scriptural witness to Joseph, we begin this review of the testimony of Tradition with a "buyer beware" warning. Too often popular articles assert that serious theological inquiry into St. Joseph did not begin until the fifteenth century (with the expositions of theologians like Jean Gerson). This is simply wrong. The essential framework for the development of doctrine and devotion relating to St. Joseph was laid out in the first five centuries of Christianity. It is this framework that served as the foundation for the magnificent edifice that has since been built. And the framework, in essence, comprises the recognition that Joseph was truly married to Mary, that he was truly the father of Jesus and that he was a virginal father.

To be sure, there were formidable obstacles to these breakthroughs. On the one hand you had the apocryphal works like the Protoevangelium that denied all three scriptural insights. And, on the other, you had critics like Helvidius who denied the perpetual virginity of the Virgin Mother. But just as great theologians arose to refute the major heresies addressed by the early Church Councils – Athanasius against Arius, Cyril of Alexandria against Nestorius – so also the errors relating to Joseph and Mary were refuted by outstanding thinkers, principally Jerome (d. 420) and Augustine (d. 430). Origen (d.254), Athanasius (d.373), Basil the Great (d. circa 380) and Ambrose (d. 397) had defended the perpetual virginity of Mary in previous centuries and this truth was formally defined in the Second Council of Constantinople (553): "the Word of God came down from the heavens and was made flesh of holy and glorious Mary, mother of God and *ever-virgin*, and was born from her."

In considering the biblical record pertaining to Joseph, we encountered the question of interpretation. What we call "tradition", in a sense, includes the interpretation of what is given in the public revelation. But it is significant inasmuch as it is considered an authoritative interpretation, one guided by the same Spirit who inspired the Scriptures.

This authoritative interpretation undergirds the development of doctrine. Not only is the Bible not a textbook of science but it is not a textbook of doctrine. But there is no Christianity without doctrine – authoritative doctrine – and doctrine came to us from the Fathers, the Councils and the Church's magisterium. All the distinctive doctrines of Christianity emerged in this fashion.

As has already been said, theologically and chronologically development of doctrine as it pertains to Joseph could only come after a definitive and comprehensive articulation of the Church's understanding of Jesus and Mary. In Scripture, the revelation of Jesus' identity as Son of the Father meant that there could be no confusion between the earthly father and the heavenly Father. Thus, by the time of Jesus' public ministry, Joseph was no longer alive. Moreover, it was emphasized that the earthly father was not the biological father.

In subsequent Christian history, the focus first had to be on Christology followed (and sometimes paralleled) by Mariology. By the time the Christological and the Mariological doctrines were firmly in place, it was already the eighth century. It was only after this that the doctrinal development relating to Joseph could begin its gradual ascent.

This trajectory of doctrinal development mirrors the pattern of progress in other fields of human knowledge. Take science. With each new advancement in our knowledge of nature, we arrive at further insights. This is seen in the progressive interplay of theory and experiment that led to the Standard Model in physics. Moreover, in quantum physics, new discoveries at the sub-atomic level led to breath-taking applications in the macroscopic world. Everything is not delivered at once – rather we have to scale the slopes with perseverance and vision if we are to reach the summit.

Fr. Joseph Lienhardt notes that the early Church Fathers were concerned with four questions about Joseph: two involving biblical interpretation and two doctrine. The biblical interpretation issues related to variations in the genealogies in Luke and Matthew and the precise relationship of the brothers and sisters of Jesus. The doctrinal questions concerned whether Joseph was truly married to Mary and truly the father of Jesus.

We have reviewed the interpretation of the biblical and classical texts relating to these issues. But here we should emphasize that the authoritative interpretation we have today came relatively early in the consolidation of Christian doctrine – within the first half of the first Christian millennium. This was thanks to the work of St. Jerome (347 –420) and St. Augustine (354 –430).

Lienhard observes that "Jerome, who held that Joseph was a virgin, insisted vigorously that the brethren of the Lord were not Joseph's children but cousins of Jesus. With Jerome and Augustine a doctrinal tradition began that took root in the West and persisted there. Jerome, in his work against Helvidius written in 383, argues for Joseph's virginity by association and appropriateness." While Augustine in his early days had once speculated that Joseph had children from a first wife, he later affirmed clearly "that Joseph was perpetually a virgin. Thereafter Augustine continued to defend Joseph's purity, in Sermon 51 and his first work against Julian."[1]

Some excerpts from Augustine's Sermon 51[2] help us to see how this Father of the Church had already discerned the fundamental infrastructure of doctrine relating to St. Joseph

> That the generations of Christ are counted through Joseph.] Now the Scripture is intent on showing that he was not born of Joseph's seed, when he is told in his trouble as to her being with child, "He is of the Holy Ghost"; and yet his paternal authority is not taken from him, forasmuch as he is commanded to name the child; and again the Virgin Mary herself, who was well aware that it was not by him that she conceived Christ, yet calls him the father of Christ.

> Jesus subject to his parents
> [On Lk 2:49] The answer then of the Lord Jesus Christ, "I must be about my Father's

service," does not in such sense declare God to be his Father, as to deny that Joseph was his father also.... "He came to Nazareth and was subject to them." It did not say, "He was subject to his mother," or was "subject to her," but "He was subject to them." To whom was he subject? Was it not to his parents? It was to both his parents that he was subject, by the same condescension by which he was the Son of Man.

Joseph and Mary were Jesus' parents in time

They were his parents in time, God was his father eternally. They were the parents of the Son of Man.

Joseph a father in chastity

As that then was a true marriage, and a marriage free from all corruption, so why should not the husband chastely receive what his wife had chastely brought forth? For as she was a wife in chastity, so was he in chastity a husband; and as she was in chastity a mother, so was he in chastity a father. Whoever then says that he ought not to be called father, because he did not beget his son in the usual way, looks rather to the satisfaction of passion in the procreation of children, and not the natural feeling of affection. What others desire to fulfill in the flesh, he in a more excellent way fulfilled in the spirit.

Joseph was a most excellent father
> Not only then must Joseph be a father, but in a most excellent manner a father. For men beget children of women also who are not their wives, and they are called natural children, and the children of the lawful marriage are placed above them. Now as to the manner of their birth, they are born alike; why then are the latter set above the other, but because of the love of a wife, of whom children are born, is the more pure? The union of the sexes is not regarded in this case, for this is the same in both women. Where has the wife the preeminence but in her fidelity, her wedded love, her more true and pure affection? If then a man could have children by his wife without this intercourse, should he not have so much the more joy thereby, in proportion to the greater chastity of her whom he loves the most?

Lienhard concludes that "what the Fathers do is to establish, in bare outline, Joseph's place in the mystery of salvation. The answers to the two exegetical questions posed earlier cleared the way for doctrinal development. The Fathers taught that Jesus indeed the Son of David and that the so-called brothers and sisters of Jesus were not the children of Mary.

They key point about Jesus' ancestry is not Joseph's bloodline but Jesus' Davidic sonship, and the gospels posed no obstacle to affirming that Davidic sonship. And further, the 'brothers and sisters of Jesus' were not an obstacle to affirming Mary's perpetual virginity. Further doctrinal development followed three points: the gospels' statement that Joseph was a just man, the dignity of Joseph and Mary, and Joseph's personal authority in regard to Jesus."[3]

It must be admitted that not all the Fathers of the Church shared these insights. The *Protoevangelium* and other apocryphal works unfortunately influenced several of the Eastern Fathers. But it should also be said that any pronouncements they made about St. Joseph are based not on their reflection on Scripture but on historically and theologically unreliable and demonstrably inaccurate documents. This was not the case with the reflections of Jerome and Augustine. Lienhard cites examples not just from Jerome and Augustine but also Ambrose, Origen and John Chrysostom. It is their contributions that served as the template for the development of doctrine and devotion concerning St. Joseph and the Holy Family.

Paradoxically, despite the influence of the apocrypha, doctrine and devotion relating to St. Joseph rose most rapidly in the East. The famous St. Ephrem of Syria (306-372) composed the earliest paean to

St. Joseph: "Blessed are you, O just Joseph, for He who became a child grew up at your side taking you for His model; (The Word) lived under your roof, though never leaving the Father. Blessed are the names He has taken in his love: He who was the Son of the Father is called son of David, son of Joseph. No one will ever be able to praise Joseph worthily except You Yourself who are truly and according to nature the Son of the Eternal Father, You the loving shepherd whose mission has always been the perpetual following after the sheep in danger of perishing."[4]

The first feast of St. Joseph (July 20th) was instituted in Egypt in the seventh century. It is touching indeed that the land that welcomed him during his earthly sojourn was also the first to "receive" him into their ecclesial heart after his celestial homecoming. In fact, Egypt's own apocryphal work, *The History of Joseph the Carpenter* (late sixth century), while repeating the errors of the other apocrypha, nevertheless has a remarkable tribute from Jesus to Joseph at the time of his death: "The smell or corruption of death shall not have dominion over you, nor shall a worm ever come forth from your body. Not a single limb of it shall be broken, nor shall any hair on your head be changed. Nothing of your body shall perish, O my father Joseph, but it will remain entire and uncorrupted even until the banquet of the thousand years. And whosoever shall make an offering on the day of your remembrance, him will I bless and recompense."⁵

Also noteworthy is the portrait of the pre-Apocrypha St. Joseph. Michael Griffin points out that "It is interesting to note that that the earliest known paintings or pieces of sculpture in the catacombs show Joseph as a young man, probably no more than twenty-five years old. This trend continued until the fourth century." Only in later art was he portrayed as an octogenarian. "There can be no doubt that the change was deliberately introduced.... Portraying him as a very old man, they [the artists] thought, was the best way of upholding belief in the perpetual virginity of Mary and Joseph." Fortunately, this portrayal has been reversed in modern times. "This healthy trend accords with modern scriptural scholarship and has helped thinking Christians to reject as worthless fables many of the legends about Saint Joseph that are contained in the apocryphal literature."⁶

Lienhard concludes that "Interest in St. Joseph, and devotion to him, have grown rapidly since the fifteenth century. In elaborating that devotion, however, the Church did not innovate but drew on Scripture and on the traditions about Joseph found in the writings of the Fathers."⁷

The Saints' Saint

The consensus of the faithful is that Mary is the greatest of the saints, in fact the Queen of all saints. But who comes after her and, for that matter, is there a hierarchy in the communion of saints? Over the centuries, the saints themselves pointed to St. Joseph as the greatest saint after Mary. It is quite remarkable that it is not simply the Church that proclaims St. Joseph as Patron of the Universal Church and Heavenly Protector but he was christened as such by the saints of the Church. The Fathers and Doctors of the Church had pondered the mystery of Joseph's marriage to Mary and his fatherhood of Jesus. This laid the framework for the later development of doctrine and devotion. As a result, by the time of St. Bernard of Clairvaux (1090 –1153) in the twelfth century, the unimaginably significant dignity of St. Joseph's office became too obvious to ignore.

In a famous meditation on Joseph, Bernard writes:

> Joseph's character and qualities can be deduced from the fact that God honored him with the title of father, and, although his doing so was a mere matter of convenience, this was what he was known as and believed to be. Joseph's own name, which, as you know means "increase,"

supplies further indications. Call to mind the great patriarch of old who was sold into Egypt, and you will realize that it was not only his name that our saint received but also his chastity, innocence, and grace.

His brothers' envy had caused the earlier Joseph to be sold and taken to Egypt, thus symbolizing the selling of Christ: the later Joseph carried Christ into Egypt, fleeing before Herod's envy. The former Joseph kept faith with his master and would not become involved with his master's wife, while his namesake faithfully protected his own spouse, the mother of his Lord, acknowledging her virginity and remaining continent himself. The first Joseph had the gift of interpreting dreams: the second was given a revelation of the divine plan and a share in its accomplishment. Joseph the patriarch stored up grain, not for himself but for all the people: our Joseph was given custody of the living bread from heaven to keep safe both for himself and the whole world.

There is no doubt that the Joseph to whom the Savior's mother was engaged was a good and faithful man. He was, I say, the wise and faithful steward whom the Lord appointed to support his mother and care for himself in childhood, singling him out for his complete reliability to help him with his momentous plan.

Added to all this, scripture tells us that he was of David's house. Joseph was obviously of David's house, a true descendant of the royal line, a man of noble birth and still nobler disposition. That he was David's son was seen from the fact that he in no way failed to maintain his standard: he was a true son of David not only as regards physical descent, but also in his faith, holiness, and devotion. In him the Lord found, as it were, a second David, a man after his own heart, to whom he could safely confide his most holy and secret design. To him as to another David he revealed the unfathomable, hidden depths of his wisdom, and granted him knowledge of that mystery which was known to none of the princes of this world. In a word, that which many kings and prophets had longed to see and had not seen, to hear and had not heard -that was granted to Joseph. He was allowed not only to see and hear him, but also to carry him, guide his steps, embrace and kiss him, cherish and protect him.[1]

Saint Bernard also said: "There are some saints who have the power of protecting in certain specific circumstances; but Saint Joseph has been granted the power to help us in every kind of need, and to defend all who have recourse to him with pious dispositions."[2]

The greatest exponent of devotion to St. Joseph among the saints was St. Teresa of Avila (1515 –1582). She carried out her hard-fought reformation of the Carmelite order under the patronage of St. Joseph. Her personal testimony in her autobiography to the power of St. Joseph's intercession is an enduring and moving masterpiece:

> I took for my advocate and lord the glorious Saint Joseph and commended myself earnestly to him; and I found that this my father and lord delivered me both from this trouble and also from other and greater troubles concerning my honor and the loss of my soul, and that he gave me greater blessings than I could ask of him. I do not remember even now that I have ever asked anything of him which he has failed to grant. I am astonished at the great favors which God has bestowed on me through this blessed saint, and at the perils from which He has freed me, both in body and in soul. To other saints the Lord seems to have given grace to succor us in some of our necessities but of this glorious saint my experience is that he succors us in them all and that the Lord wishes to teach

us that as He was Himself subject to him on earth (for, being His guardian and being called His father, he could command Him) just so in Heaven He still does all that he asks. This has also been the experience of other persons whom I have advised to commend themselves to him; and even to-day there are many who have great devotion to him through having newly experienced this truth....

I wish I could persuade everyone to be devoted to this glorious saint, for I have great experience of the blessings which he can obtain from God. I have never known anyone to be truly devoted to him and render him particular services who did not notably advance in virtue, for he gives very real help to souls who commend themselves to him. For some years now, I think, I have made some request of him every year on his festival and I have always had it granted. If my petition is in any way ill directed, he directs it aright for my greater good....

I only beg, for the love of God, that anyone who does not believe me will put what I say to the test, and he will see by experience what great advantages come from his commending himself to this glorious patriarch and having devotion to him. Those who practice prayer should have a special affection for him always. I do not know how anyone can think of the Queen of the Angels, during the time that she suffered so much with the Child Jesus, without giving thanks to Saint Joseph for the way he helped them. If anyone cannot find a master to teach him how to pray, let him take this glorious saint as his master and he will not go astray.[3]

Devotees of St. Joseph include a Who's Who of the saints of the second millennium:

St. Dominic (1170 – 1221)
St. Francis of Assisi (1181 – 1226)
St. Thomas Aquinas (1225 – 1274)
St. Gertrude (1256 –1302)
St. Bridget (1303 –1373)
St. Catherine of Siena (1347 – 1380)
St. Bernardine of Siena (1380 – 1444)
St. Ignatius of Loyola (1491– 1556)
St. John of the Cross (1542 – 1591)
St. Francis de Sales (1567 –1622)
St. Alphonsus Ligouri (1696–1787)
St. Bernadette (1844 – 1879)
St. Therese of Lisieux. (1873 – 1897)

Especially noteworthy for their insight into St. Joseph are these excerpts from the saints:

St. Thomas Aquinas

"Some Saints are privileged to extend to us their patronage with particular efficacy in certain needs, but not in others; but our holy patron St. Joseph has the power to assist us in all cases, in every necessity, in every undertaking."

St. Bernardine of Siena

There is a general rule concerning all special graces granted to any human being. Whenever the divine favor chooses someone to receive a special grace, or to accept a lofty vocation, God adorns the person chosen with all the gifts of the Spirit needed to fulfill the task at hand. This general rule is especially verified in the case of Saint Joseph, the foster-father of our Lord, and the husband of the Queen of our world, enthroned above the angels. He was chosen by the eternal Father as the trustworthy guardian and protector of his greatest treasures, namely, his divine Son and Mary, Joseph's wife. He carried out this vocation with complete fidelity until at last God called him, saying "Good and faithful servant, enter into the joy of your Lord." Remember us, Saint Joseph, and plead for us to your foster child. Ask your most holy bride, the Virgin Mary, to look kindly upon us, since she is the mother of him who with the Father and the Holy Spirit lives and reigns eternally. Amen.

St. Francis de Sales
"Our Blessed Lady and her glorious Son will refuse Joseph nothing"[4]

St. Peter Julian Eymard
Behold, the beautiful month of St. Joseph!....Aside from the Blessed Virgin, Saint Joseph was the first and most perfect adorer of our Lord. Faith, humility, purity, and love - these were the keynotes of his adoration.

Devotion to Saint Joseph is one of the choicest graces that God can give to a soul, for it is tantamount to revealing the entire treasury of our Lord's graces. But only our Lord can reveal him to us, for he is hidden away....

God has bestowed upon Saint Joseph a special mission in the Church....Is he not the chosen one who enabled Christ to enter into the world according to the laws of order...? Next to [the Virgin Mary], the Church owes her greatest debt of gratitude and veneration to Saint Joseph, for he is the key to the Old Testament. It is by him that the patriarchs and the prophets reaped the fruit of God's promise. Alone among them all, Joseph saw with his own eyes and possessed the Redeemer promised to the rest of men....

Saint Joseph, the greatest of saints after Mary, suffered more than all the saints...The source of his suffering lay in his deep, tender, and enlightened love for Jesus and in his veneration for the Virgin Mary.… Only in heaven will we shall we grasp the full extent of Saint Joseph's suffering; but what we already know from meditation helps us to estimate his merits and the intensity of his love."

St. Bridget of Sweden reported that the Blessed Virgin Mary said this about her husband:

"St. Joseph was so reserved and careful in his speech that not one word ever issued from his mouth that was not good and holy, nor did he ever indulge in unnecessary or less than charitable conversation. He was most patient and diligent in bearing fatigue; he practiced extreme poverty; he was most meek in bearing injuries; he was strong and constant against my enemies; he was the faithful witness of the wonders of Heaven, being dead to the flesh and the world, living only for God and for Heavenly goods, which were the only things he desired. He was perfectly conformed to the Divine Will and so resigned to the dispositions of Heaven that he ever repeated 'May the Will of God ever be done in me!' He rarely spoke with men, but continually with God, whose Will he desired to perform. Wherefore, he now enjoys great glory in Heaven."

A Prophecy

Isidore of Isolanis, a 16th century Dominican, prophesied that "toward the end of time God will overwhelm St. Joseph with glorious honors. If in the past ages, during the storms of persecution, these honors could not be shown to St. Joseph, we must conclude that they have been reserved for later times. At some future time the feast of St. Joseph will be celebrated as one of the greatest of feasts. The Vicar of Christ, inspired by the Holy Spirit, will order this feast to be celebrated in the Universal Church."[5]

Theological Momentum

The renewed theological attention to the Joseph of the Gospels and the liberation from the legends of the apocrypha began with Jean Gerson, Chancellor of the University of Paris (1363-1429). The two greatest theologians of the Church – St. Augustine and St. Thomas Aquinas – had already laid the foundations for a theological understanding of the role of St. Joseph. They held that:

- ❖ Joseph was a "just man" in the sense of a holy man,
- ❖ he was truly the husband of Mary,
- ❖ he was truly and virginally the father of Jesus because he was the husband of Mary
- ❖ he exercised paternal authority over Jesus.

From these hard facts of biblical revelation arose the entire edifice of Josephine theology and devotion.

St. Thomas consolidated the insights articulated by Augustine by laying out twelve theological reasons for the true marriage of Joseph and Mary and then goes further. Fr. Basil Cole writes,

> "St. Thomas Aquinas gives us three very important theological principles that can help in interpreting not only the life of St. Joseph,

but also the lives of the saints as well. The first is that when God chooses someone for a special mission in the Church, he always prepares that person with many graces, and sometimes gifts of nature to fulfill that task (ST III 98, 5 ad 3). From this we may draw the conclusion that since Joseph was to be the head of the Holy Family, a ministry much higher than being a priest or pope because Joseph was immediately in charge of Christ himself and married to Mary, he had to be capacitated with exceptional graces for these purposes. It is argued by many Josephine scholars that Joseph, while not immaculately conceived, was sanctified in the womb by the grace of God like John the Baptist and Jeremiah.

The second insight of Aquinas that helps us understand Joseph's holiness is that the more one approaches the principle of grace, the more one receives the effects from that principle *(ibid.,* 5; see also II-II 1, 7 ad 4). In Joseph's case, this would mean receiving an ocean of grace because Joseph lived with Jesus, the head of the mystical body as well as Mary, the Queen of heaven and earth, the sinless one. From this it follows that Joseph would have been inundated with grace throughout his life thus enabling him to live and merit not only his own salvation but also the salvation of others. This is the source of his special role in heaven as patron of the Universal Church.

As a third rationale, St. Thomas teaches that the virtue of devotion, an aspect of the virtue of religion being a willingness to serve God more readily, comes about as a result of meditation and contemplation. Principally pondering and gazing concerns itself with the divine nature itself as containing the infinite attributes and properties of the three-personed God (ST II-II 82, 3 ad 2). Secondarily, however, devotion arises from thinking lovingly on Jesus Christ, and his life and death. Therefore, reflecting on the mystery of Joseph aids one to think about Christ, and then helps one grow in devotion to the Triune God."[1]

The distinguished 20th century Thomist philosopher Reginald Garrigou-Lagrange further developed the insights of St. Thomas:

"No one is greater among the saints after the Mother of the Savior.

But what is the principle of this doctrine about the excellence of St. Joseph, admitted for the last five centuries? It is that proportionate sanctity is required for an exceptional divine mission, as in the case of Christ, His holy Mother, the apostles, founders of orders, and others who are immediately chosen by God.

But Joseph was predestined for an exceptional mission, one that is unique in the world and throughout all time, namely, that he should be the spouse of the Blessed Virgin Mary, the foster father of the Son of God, and that he should have in the guardianship of the Word incarnate the heart of a father, full of benevolence and love. There is nothing more exalted after the dignity of divine motherhood. Therefore St. Joseph received sanctity in proportion to this mission, and this sanctity increased until the end of his life."[2]

The bare facts about Joseph that we find in Scripture show us that the Incarnation is inescapably rooted in a family. Michael Griffin points out that "The Eternal Son of God was conceived in the womb of the Blessed Virgin, not by the power of man, but by the work of the Holy Spirit. In becoming man, Christ was born and received into a human because he wanted to be become like unto us in all things, sin alone excepted. One of the main reasons why Christ was born into a family was due to the fact that it is in accordance with the divine natural law that children should be born to a married couple."[3]

It might be asked how a mere mortal could presume to exercise authority over the Son of God. Griffin explains that "Saint Joseph exercised authority over Jesus only because this was the will of God. Obviously the right of authority can be exercised only over a person, and since Christ is a divine Person no one can have any authority over Him. The authority exercised by Joseph was given by God because Christ *chose* to be subject to His earthly father, who was the "shadow of His heavenly Father." If Jesus' humble subjection gives us an example of due submission to lawfully constituted authority, it also serves to emphasize the dignity of him whom He obeyed."[4]

The fatherhood of St. Joseph, as we have seen, was unique:

> "In the whole course of human history there has never been a type of fatherhood that is identical to that of St. Joseph. Why is this so? An event occurred in the life of Saint Joseph that has never occurred, and never will occur, to any other married men. This tremendous event implied (1) that Almighty God miraculously enabled his wife virginally to conceive and bring forth a son; (2) the child in question was the Incarnated Word of God; (3) all this occurred in such a way, according to the special designs

of Divine Providence, that the Child was not a stranger to Saint Joseph, but the fruit of his own marriage; (4) and finally Joseph by the same divine decree was, in a true sense, granted the right and duties of fatherhood towards this Child....

What is also unique in this case is the fact that the marriage of Mary and Joseph was ordained by God to receive the Son of God into the world. The Incarnate Word of God was the fruit of the marriage of the holy couple. Christ was not a stranger to their marriage....

Hence, just as Mary became the Mother of God not 'because of the will of man but because of the will of God', so neither did Joseph received his fatherhood towards Christ except by the will of God."[5]

Given St. Joseph's exalted role in the salvific scheme, the obvious question is how the faithful should "interact" with him. This leads to the distinction between adoration, directed only to God, and veneration, directed to the saints. Many of those who reject the communion of saints so clearly laid out in the Scriptures, end up venerating God while denying him adoration and sacrifice.

We have already raised the issue of intercession and mediation and will explore these in more detail here. We consider mediation first followed by intercession.

Human Mediation

Predestination to Salvation and Damnation vs. Freedom of the Human Person

The question of mediation and intercession, whether of Mary or of anyone else, is not simply a Protestant-Catholic controversy. Its roots reach down to two entirely different views of God and humankind. On the one side you have the Calvinists and other determinists and on the other you have Catholics, Orthodox, Protestants from various denominations (like the Methodists) and movements (Pentecostals) and all those who believe in human freedom. Calvinism is not the standard position even among Evangelicals as illustrated by the anthology of Evangelical scholars titled *The Grace of God, The Will of Man*.

The Calvinist, determinist view was well summarized by John Calvin himself in his "Predestination of Some to Salvation and Others to Destruction": "All things being at God's disposal, and the decision of salvation or death belonging to him, he orders all things by his counsel and decree in such a manner, that some men are born devoted from the womb to certain death, that his name may be glorified in their destruction.... No one can deny that God foreknew the future final fate of man before he created him, and that he did foreknow it because it was appointed by his own decree."[6] "The wicked themselves have been created for this very end – that they may perish."[7]

Martin Luther adopted the Calvinist view although he was clearly troubled by it: "Doubtless it gives the greatest possible offence to common sense or natural reason, that God, Who is proclaimed as being full of mercy and goodness, and so on, should of His own mere will abandon, harden, and damn men, as though He delighted in the sins and great eternal torments of such wretches.... I have stumbled at it myself more than once, down to the deepest pit of despair."[8]

The historic Christian response to this line of thought was well summed up by John Wesley in his "Predestination Calmly Considered," the most extraordinary extant refutation of Calvinism, "Now if man be capable of choosing good or evil, then is he a proper object of the justice of God, acquitting or condemning, rewarding or punishing. But otherwise he is not. A mere machine is not capable of being either acquitted or condemned. Justice cannot punish a stone for falling to the ground.... And shall this man, for not doing what he never could do, and for doing what he never could avoid, be sentenced to depart into everlasting fire, prepared for the devil and his angels (cf. Mt. 25:41)? 'Yes, because it is the sovereign will of God.' Then you either found a new God, or made one! This is not the God of the Christians. Our God is just in all his ways.... He requireth only according to what he hath given; and where he hath given little, little is required. The glory of his justice is this, to 'reward every man according to his works.' (cf. Tm 4:14)."[9]

The Council of Orange had declared in 529 "We not only do not believe that any are foreordained to evil by the power of God, but even state with utter abhorrence that if there are those who want to believe so evil a thing, they are anathema."

As long as you take the Calvinist view of the matter, which Luther did, there can be no further progression on mediation. But, as Anglican John Macquarrie points out, this view is at odds of both human experience and Christian doctrine and experience because it treats "human beings like sheep or cattle or even marionettes, not as the unique beings that they are, spiritual beings made in the image of God and entrusted with a measure of freedom and responsibility."[10].

Catholics and Protestants agree that redemption was freely secured and bestowed by Jesus Christ and accepted in faith by the believer, that God's grace takes primacy over every human initiative and that we are able to live as the children of God only because of the gift of the Holy Spirit. Disagreement arises over whether or not we can freely say yes or no to God's gift of grace. Unlike the Calvinist position, the historic Christian consensus is that God is an infinite Lover who thirsts for every human soul, that he moves Heaven and Earth to make salvation available to his creatures, that he gives every person sufficient grace to say *fiat*, "yes", to him. We can say "yes" to God because of the grace He gives us to say "yes." But we can also say "no" – and this is a free act.

The main foundation for the doctrine that our free decisions determine our eternal destiny is the teaching of Jesus in all the Gospels: "For the Son of Man is going to come in the glory of his Father with his angels, and, when he does, he will reward each one according to his behavior." (*Matthew* 16:27). This is a teaching that is reiterated in the rest of the New Testament. Says St. Paul, "Your stubborn refusal to repent is only adding to the anger God will have toward you on that day of anger when his just judgments will be made known. He will repay each one as his works deserve. For those who sought renown and honor and immortality by always doing good there will be eternal life; for the unsubmissive who refused to take truth for their guide and took depravity instead, there will be anger and fury." (*Romans* 2:5-8).

Delving deeper, we find that mediation is fundamental to Christianity:

Mediators in the Old and New Testaments

Both Old and New Testaments not only show the significance of our free acts but the very real role of mediators in God's scheme of salvation. Adam, Noah, Abraham and Moses, the Prophets, Judges and Kings of the Old Testaments, were all mediators between God and humanity. Their free actions could bring divine blessings on their people. They could cause or avert God's wrath. Things are no different in the New Testament. The Apostles and disciples are chosen and commissioned to spread the Good News, to bring people to salvation, to celebrate the sacred mysteries that "transmit" the grace of God. In a startling passage, St. Paul writes that "It makes me happy to suffer for you, as I am suffering now, and in my own body to do what I can to make up all that has still to be undergone by Christ for the sake of his body, the Church." (*Colossians* 1:24).

The One Mediator

1 Timothy 2:5 says, "There is only one mediator between God and mankind, himself a man, Christ Jesus, who sacrificed himself as a ransom for them all." Does "one" here mean "exclusively one" or does it mean "the same" and by extension "primary"? Interestingly, the Greek word used for "exclusively one", *monos*, is used in every other instance of "one" in the epistle except in this verse. The word used here is "*heis*" where it means "sameness" of function. In his study of *Timothy* 2:5, "For there is one God, and one mediator between God and men, the man Christ Jesus; Who gave himself a ransom for all," Manuel Miguens points out that an accurate translation of this passage is "There is one and the same God [for all], there is also one and the same mediator [for all]." The author is not trying to show that there is one and not a multiplicity of gods or that there is one and not many mediators. His point, rather, is that God's love and providence applies to all not just to a few (the Jews, for instance) just as the redemptive mediation of Jesus is for all. In his epistles, St. Paul, of course, talks of himself as a mediator and even talks of three kinds of mediators: priestly (Aaron, Christ), covenantal (Moses, Jesus) and de facto

mediators (Abraham and Paul). The last category comprises those chosen to be vehicles of divine grace. The mediation of all Christians (as described in Colossians 1:24 and elsewhere) is a participation in the unique and primary mediation of Christ. He alone is the unique Son of God - but all Christians can and must participate in this Sonship as they can and must participate in his unique Priesthood. So also, all are called to participate in the unique mediation of the Primary Mediator. All followers of Jesus participate in his work of salvation. St. James even says "Anyone who can bring back a sinner from the wrong way that he has taken will be saving a soul from death and covering up a great number of sins." (*James* 5:20). "We are co-workers with God," said St. Paul.

Intercession

With respect to intercession, we note that the larger question here concerns whether or not a person in Heaven can affect events on earth. We can address these issues by consideration of four different issues.

1. Perseverance in prayer is commended in Scripture with the promise that this will achieve results.

"He said, 'There was a judge in a certain town who neither feared God nor respected any human being. And a widow in that town used to come to him and say, 'Render a just decision for me against my adversary.' For a long time the judge was unwilling, but eventually he thought, 'While it is true that I neither fear God nor respect any human being, because this widow keeps bothering me I shall deliver a just decision for her lest she finally come and strike me.' The Lord said, 'Pay attention to what the dishonest judge says. Will not God the secure the rights of his chosen ones who call out to him day and night? Will he be slow to answer them? I tell you, he will see to it that justice is done for them speedily.'" (*Luke* 18:2-8).

2. Intercessory prayer from multiple persons will achieve results.

"Peter thus was being kept in prison, but prayer by the church was fervently being made to God on his behalf." (*Acts* 12:5).

"First of all, then, I ask that supplications, prayers, petitions, and thanksgivings be offered for everyone, for kings and for all in authority, that we may lead a quiet and tranquil life in all devotion and dignity. This is good and pleasing to God our savior, who wills everyone to be saved and to come to knowledge of the truth." (1 *Timothy* 2:1-5).

"As you help us with prayer, so that thanks may be given by many on our behalf for the gift granted us through the prayers of many." (2 *Cor* 1:11).

3. The prayer of a holy person is especially effective

"The fervent prayer of a righteous person is very powerful." (*James* 5:16).

4. The prayer of the Holy Ones in Heaven has an effect on earthly events.

"When he took it, the four living creatures and the twenty-four elders fell down before the Lamb. Each of the elders held a harp and gold bowls filled with incense, which are the prayers of the holy ones." (*Revelation* 5:8). The elders in this instance are Christians in Heaven. "The smoke of the incense along with the prayers of the holy ones went up before God from the hand of the angel." (*Revelation* 8:4). "I saw underneath the altar the souls of those who had been slaughtered because of the witness they bore to the word of God. They cried out in a loud voice, 'How long will it be, holy and true master, before you sit in judgment and avenge our blood on the inhabitants of the earth?' Each of them was given a white robe, and they were told to be patient a little while longer until the number was filled of their fellow servants and brothers who were going to be killed as they had been." (*Revelation* 6:9-11).

The Anglican theologian Edward Symonds observes that "There are other considerations however in favour of the view that the saints hear us. There is actual evidence for this belief in the New Testament. Heb 12:1 says: 'Therefore let us also being compassed about with so great a cloud of witnesses ("martyrs", alluding to the heroes of faith in the preceding chapter) run with patience ("endurance") the race which is set before us', where the witnesses, though primarily witnesses to their faith suggest at least, as Westcott points out, 'spectators' looking on at our earthly struggle in running the race appointed for us Christians. This is confirmed by the picture of the heavenly Jerusalem in the same chapter to which Christians on earth are now come, with the solemn assembly of the firstborn and the spirits of just men made perfect. (Verse 23)."[11]

Devotional Crescendo

The deepening insight into St. Joseph's place in the Christian scheme of things was not simply intellectual. Historically, greater clarity in matters of doctrine opened the floodgates to an outpouring of devotion from the faithful. The proclamation of the divinity of Jesus at Nicea and the declaration of the Divine Maternity at Ephesus, for instance, both had an immediate impact in terms of liturgical celebration and popular piety. Equally, the devotional fervor of the faithful has often helped the Church discern the direction of the Most High – a teaching activity that had to be exercised, however, with the greatest care. For the discernment of Christian truth requires not simply head and heart but the Holy Spirit.

At any rate, the witness of Scripture, Church Fathers and Doctors, saints and theologians to the Josephine patrimony was matched by a spiritual outburst of love from both clergy and laity. It manifested itself in the devotions and practices of the saints, the testimonies of the mystics, the heart-to-heart encounters of believers with their spiritual father and, finally, the litanies, prayers and feasts instituted by the Church.

Ancient Devotion

Late though it came in the West, the devotional response of the faithful to St. Joseph received its initial impetus at the epicenter of ancient Christianity, namely Central Asia, within the Eastern Church. This is astonishing given the negative influence of the apocrypha in the East. But the workings of Providence are paradoxical.

Appropriately enough, as already noted, this pilgrimage of faith began in Egypt, the very land to which the "just man" brought his family: "The first feast day of S. Joseph was reputedly kept by the Copts from the beginning of the 4th century AD, and a feast of S. Joseph the Carpenter is certainly entered, on the 20th July, in the oldest Coptic calendars known to scholars. S. Joseph's early appearance in the devotions of Egyptian Christians is probably due to his important role in one of the Biblical narratives most cherished by the Copts: The exile of the Holy Family to Egypt. Countless popular legends have grown up around the Exile, with many monasteries, churches and shrines in Egypt positioned somewhere along the projected route taken by the Holy Family. To this day one can visit, in S. Sergius Church in Old Cairo, a grotto where the Holy Family took shelter."[1]

The 19th century writer Edward Healy Thompson provides a striking glimpse of the devotional life of the early Eastern Church:

> In the East especially we meet with proofs that devotion to St. Joseph was cherished from the earliest, that is, from Apostolic times, and many traditions of him were current in these regions. Papebrock, one of the continuators of the Bollandists, says that St. Joseph was honoured among the Egyptians, and his feast kept in the primitive ages of Christianity, even before the times of St. Athanasius, that is, in the beginning of the fourth century; so that Trombelli, following Papebrock, concludes that, from the traditional recollection of the Saint's sojourn in those countries, he was venerated there long before St. Athanasius sent missionaries to instruct the inhabitants in the rites and discipline of the Church of Alexandria. In Syria and Persia also we find traces of early honour paid to St. Joseph; and in the Greek Church … we have monuments of it from the time of Constantine the Great, and even earlier still. Martorelli says, "The site of an ancient oratory dedicated to St. Joseph is still pointed out on the slope of the hill between the Grotto of Milk and the Great Church of the Holy Crib, afterwards built by St. Helen,

mother of Constantine". In that sumptuous basilica, as Nicephorus Callistus testifies in his Ecclesiastical history (quoted by Martorelli), was a magnificent chapel, or oratory, sacred to St. Joseph. In several of the Eastern menologies we find mention of St. Joseph. Thus in the menology of the Greeks, published by Cardinal Sirleto, we find these words on the 26th of December: "The celebrity, or solemn memory, of Our Holy Lady Mother of God, the Ever-Virgin Mary, and of the holy and just Joseph, her spouse". According to Assemani, also, St. Joseph is mentioned in the menology of the Emperor Basil and other Greek menologies on the 25th and 26th of December, and on the Sundays before and after the Nativity of our Lord. The ancient hymns of the Greek Church likewise bear witness to the honour paid to St. Joseph.[2]

A more recent overview of that early era comes from the Oblates of St. Joseph:

> The Coptic church in Egypt links the figure of Joseph to the journey of the Holy Family there to purify the idols, to fulfill the Old Testament prophecies and to bless their land. It seems to be this ... that developed into the most ancient feast of St. Joseph, that of his

passing or death…. Coptic Egyptians still celebrate this feast in their monasteries Abîb 26 (July 20 in the old Julian calendar)…. An Ethiopian Synaxary similarly states that for the 26th of their month Hamlê: "On this day died at a good old age the righteous man Joseph, the carpenter, who was worthy to be called the father of Christ in the flesh, and concerning whom the Holy Gospel bears witness that he was a righteous man, and that because of this our Lady Saint Mary was in safe keeping with him." For the 16th of the month Sanê, it also reads at the end: "And on this day the angel of God appeared to Joseph in a dream, and told him to take the Child and His mother, and to return to the land of Israel."

Tenth-century calendars in the East compiled in the Palestinian monastery of St. Saba mention the feast of St. Joseph. The menology (liturgical calendar of saints) of Basil II commemorates St. Joseph on the actual day of Christmas, and the flight into Egypt on the following day.

Other Synaxaries celebrate on December 26 a feast of Mary and her husband Joseph; on the Sunday before Christmas the feast of Jesus' ancestors from Abraham to Joseph, the husband of Mary; and on the Sunday within the octave of Christmas the feast of St. Joseph together with king David and James the brother of the Lord. Early on, in the Greek Church there are found beautiful hymns and prayers honoring St. Joseph as a sharer in the supreme mysteries entrusted only to him, Gabriel and Mary, and hidden from the Prince of Darkness. He is called a living, shining temple of the Creator, for his zeal in the works of God. His virtues are meekness, justice, obedience and purity.

The churches of Syrian origin have a feast that is closer to being an exclusively Josephite feast. For Maronite Catholics the second Sunday before Christmas is the "Sunday of the Revelation to Joseph," with many beautiful Josephite texts for the liturgy of the Mass and the Hours. For Chaldean Catholics this same feast of St. Joseph is celebrated on the Sunday immediately preceding Christmas.[3]

To be sure, devotion to St. Joseph appeared late in the West. There are many factors to blame for this: the influence of the apocrypha, the focus on doctrinal issues relating to Jesus and Mary, the need for a theological framework within which the devotion could be placed.

The Devotion in the West

But as the Oblates point out, popular devotions to St. Joseph are already found in the West in the eighth century.

> In the West the history of St. Joseph in the liturgy, from early times until the present, is closely linked with the history of the feast of March 19, which is long and gradual.
>
> Several examples exist listing St. Joseph in early Western martyrologies. Among these is an eighth century calendar of a Benedictine abbey of Rheinau in the Canton of Zurich, commemorating him on March 20. Another Benedictine abbey in Reichenau, southern Germany, founded in the ninth century, commemorates him on March 19 and also seems to be a forerunner for the spread of his devotion. The tenth century martyrology of Fulda has for March 19 the early title "In Bethlehem, St. Joseph, Provider for the Lord." …
>
> By about 1030 the Benedictine Abbey of Winchester was celebrating St. Joseph's feast.
>
> By 1129 the Benedictines of St. Helen constructed a church dedicated to St. Joseph at Borgo Galliera, Bologna. It seems to have been

a center from which the devotion extended far and wide. Here the name "Joseph," which was already quite common in the East, began to be given frequently to children at Baptism. It is probable that early Franciscan devotion to St. Joseph was influenced by contacts with Bologna.

In the thirteenth century we find proper texts composed to celebrate the feast. In Liege there is a proper oration to St. Joseph. The Benedictine Abbey of St. Lawrence there has a full Liturgy of the Hours in his honor, complete with musical notes. St. Florian Monastery in Austria has a missal with one Mass in honor of St. Joseph, and another "Against the calumny of wicked men," in which his merits are invoked.

The crusades, of course, were the occasion for bringing from the Holy Land supposed relics, such as St. Joseph's staff and the betrothal ring he gave Mary. In 1254 a chapel was constructed in St. Lawrence Church at Joinville sur Marne, France, to reverence his cincture, and this became a center for pilgrimage. It is likely that in the various areas where chapels sprang up in his honor, the feast of St. Joseph was celebrated in March.[4]

Religious orders like the Servites and the Franciscans began to celebrate the feast of St. Joseph in March. "At Agrigento where Franciscans, Dominicans and Carmelites were present, there is a fourteenth century "Office of Most Holy Joseph, foster and adoptive father of Our Lord Jesus Christ."

Liturgical Celebrations

By the fifteenth century, the March feast "began to take on a more universal nature. At the Council of Constance (1414-1418) the assembled bishops heard the fervent chancellor Jean Gerson preach on the powerful intercession of St. Joseph, who had commanded the child Jesus and who could be invoked efficaciously to end the schism afflicting the Church. Gerson asked the council to consider official bestowal of greater honor for St. Joseph. Franciscan influence in this century, however, seems to have been the main factor in extending the feast. Franciscans such as Bernardine of Sienna (d. 1414) not only preached on St. Joseph, but also saw the distribution of their sermon outlines." In 1471 Pope Sixtus IV allowed the March feast of St. Joseph to be celebrated locally in Rome as a feast with the same rank as that of the Epiphany, Annunciation and Easter.[5]

These raindrops of devotion gradually became a torrential downpour in 1570. Following the Council of Trent, Pope Pius X published a missal that included the March 19 feast of "St. Joseph the Confessor". With this the feast was "definitively set in the Universal Church Calendar and the cycle of the saints." Moreover "the new liturgical books certainly had the value of extending scattered popular devotions to the whole Church. Many rich texts, especially hymns and sequences in honor of St. Joseph were produced during this century in the various particular breviaries and missals published prior to those of Pius V."[6]

Several other feasts associated with St. Joseph were now celebrated within local jurisdictions of the Church:

- Feast of the espousals (January and March)
- Feast of the Patronage of the Ring (July 10)
- Feast of the Patronage of Saint Joseph (third Sunday after Easter)
- Votive Mass of St. Joseph (Mass in honor of St. Joseph which was celebrated from the thirteenth century)
- Feast of the Holy Family (January 22)
- Feast of the Flight into Egypt (fourth Sunday of April)

In 1726, Pope Benedict XIII included St. Joseph in the Litany of Saints. In 1870, based on the petitions presented at Vatican I, Pope Pius IX proclaimed St. Joseph as Patron of the Church. In 1909, Pope Pius X approved the Litany of St. Joseph. On May 1, 1955, Pope Pius XII established May 1 as the liturgical feast of St. Joseph the Worker. On November 13, 1962, Pope John XXIII announced that "and Blessed Joseph, husband of the same Virgin Mary" would be included in the canon of the Mass. In 2020, Pope Francis announced a 2020-21 Year of St. Joseph that would begin on December 8 2020.

Mystics

In parallel with these acts of the Church, several mystics published what they affirmed to be supernaturally revealed accounts of the life of St. Joseph. Perhaps the best known of these accounts are those of Blessed Mary of Agreda and Anne Katherine Emmerich. In these works, the mystics speak both of the early life of Joseph and his preparation for his exalted role and his life in the Holy Family.

The Nature of Devotion to St. Joseph

Two questions are relevant at this stage: if St. Joseph is so important in the life of the Christian, how is it that devotion to him appeared so late in history? And how is devotion to St. Joseph different from devotion to the Blessed Virgin or the other saints?

The first question applies to any of the truths of faith – to reiterate a theme we have repeatedly treated here. The divinity of Jesus and the divinity of Holy Spirit were definitively declared as dogmas of the faith only several centuries after the coming of Jesus. The declarations unpacked truths already revealed and present from the beginning. But what was implicitly present had to be made explicit authoritatively. Once this was done believers could recognize more fully the glory of the Divine Persons and offer the worship that was rightfully theirs. It is not possible to adore a Divine Person without knowing him for who he is. Those who do not know the true identity of Jesus cannot offer him the worship that is his due. Likewise, at the level of veneration of the saints, there can be no devotion to Mary or Joseph without knowing them for who they are. By the nature of the human condition, our understanding of the content of the primordial revelation of Jesus is a progressive process. We proceed from one truth to the next. Once the truth about Joseph became apparent, rightful devotion to him spread across the Christian firmament.

Turning to the second question, let us note that there are different kinds of devotion. To God we offer sacrifice and adoration. To human creatures who participated and continue to participate in God's plan of salvation, we offer a veneration that corresponds to the part they play. As has been said, Mary is the human person most involved in her Son's sacrifice of himself for the salvation of humanity. After Mary there is Joseph who was an integral part of the mission of Jesus from the start. Finally, there are the saints, those who lived and proclaimed, preached and practiced, the message of salvation.

Between adoration and sacrifice on the one hand – offered only to God – and veneration on the other – offered to human creatures who cooperated eminently with God's salvific scheme – there is an infinite gulf. The worship owed to God is called *latria* (adoration). The veneration accorded to the saints is termed *dulia* (veneration accorded to a servant). But within such veneration there are three categories: *hyperdulia*, the highest veneration, accorded only to the Blessed Virgin; *protodulia* accorded to St. Joseph, first among the saints (*proto* for first); and *dulia* accorded to the other saints.

A Global Response

We have seen that the first shoots of devotion to St. Joseph sprang in Eastern Christianity from almost the earliest days. We noted too that this devotion spread across the New World when Christianity was first introduced there in the fifteenth century. The global nature of the devotion is apparent when we consider China. St. Joseph was the Patron of the Mission in China introduced by Fr. Matteo Ricci in the sixteenth century. The parish of St. Joseph in Beijing was begun over 400 years ago. "In the Chinese Catholic world, fervent devotion to the Spouse of Mary and the guardian of the Child Jesus has a long tradition and history. Each year, the Solemnity of St. Joseph is a moment of great celebration, with prayers, novenas, Eucharistic Adoration that give great honor to the most humble Saint. For this reason, the Chinese faithful harbor a special affection for him, as evidenced by the many churches and ecclesial structures (seminaries and national and diocesan congregations), charitable institutions (orphanages, homes for the elderly), and Catholic schools that are dedicated to him and bear his name. Also, St. Joseph is also patron of a "good death", and this is resonant with the great Chinese tradition, which is very attentive to the spiritual aspects that affect life and death."[7]

Litany of St. Joseph

Authentic devotion to St. Joseph is best epitomized by the Litany of St. Joseph (below) approved by St. Pius X.

Lord, have mercy
Christ, have mercy
Lord, have mercy
God our Father in heaven, Have mercy on u
God the Son, Redeemer of the world, Have mercy on us
God the Holy Spirit, Have mercy on us
Holy Trinity, one God, Have mercy on us
Holy Mary, Pray for us
Saint Joseph, *Pray for us* [to be repeated after the titles below]
Noble son of the House of David
Light of patriarchs
Husband of the Mother of God
Guardian of the Virgin
Foster father of the Son of God
Faithful guardian of Christ
Head of the holy family
Joseph, chaste and just
Joseph, prudent and brave
Joseph, obedient and loyal
Pattern of patience
Lover of poverty

Model of workers
Example to parents
Guardian of virgins
Pillar of family life
Comfort of the troubled
Hope of the sick
Patron of the dying
Terror of evil spirits
Protector of the Church, *Pray for us.*
Lamb of God, who takest away the sins of the world, *spare us, O Lord.*
Lamb of God, who takest away the sins of the world, *graciously hear us, O Lord.*
Lamb of God, who takest away the sins of the world, *have mercy on us.*
V. He made him lord over his house,
R. And the ruler of all his possessions.
Let us pray.
God, in your infinite wisdom and love you chose Joseph to be the husband of Mary, the mother of your Son. May we have the help of his prayers in heaven and enjoy his protection on earth. We ask this through Christ our Lord. Amen.

The Church Says "Yes"

"Jesus said to him in reply, 'Blessed are you, Simon son of Jonah. For flesh and blood has not revealed this to you, but my heavenly Father. And so I say to you, you are Peter, and upon this rock I will build my church, and the gates of the netherworld shall not prevail against it. I will give you the keys to the kingdom of heaven. Whatever you bind on earth shall be bound in heaven; and whatever you loose on earth shall be loosed in heaven.'" (Matthew 16:16-19).

The unshackling from the apocryphal narratives and the re-discovery of the Joseph of the New Testament; the theological treasure-hunt for the Father of Jesus and the Husband of Mary; the insights and experiences of the faithful, the mystics and the saints; and the direct intervention of Heaven: all these bore fruit finally in the Church's resounding proclamation of St. Joseph as Patron of the Universal Church who was then included in the Canon of the Mass. The response of the Church was cautious, slow and measured but once she spoke the die was cast: there would be no going back, no further hesitation, no doubt: the case was closed, the course irreversible. It was always thus. The great Christian doctrines – the Trinity, the Incarnation, the Mother of God – were hammered out in crucibles of conceptual combat. The Church was never a "creator" of doctrine. Her role was simply to discern which of the competing interpretations was consistent with the core revelation handed down to her. There were no new "revelations": simply a deeper and more "global" understanding of the implications and applications of the same primordial revelation. But once the Church, guided by the Holy Spirit, had reached a conclusion, what she bound "on earth" was also "bound in heaven."

In the case of St. Joseph, the Church's conclusion was unmistakable and forceful. We have reviewed the Feasts, devotions and liturgical practices approved by the Church. These approvals were significant because they implicitly certified the theological truths in which they were grounded. And every Pope since Sixtus IV in 1471 has advanced the process of discernment that led to the development of doctrine and devotion as it related to St. Joseph. Of particular note is Pope John XXIII: "In four short years, Pope John gave a great deal to honor St. Joseph. A study of nearly three thousand documents of the Holy See relating to St. Joseph reveals no comparable period in the history of the devotion to St. Joseph … The peak … of the present crescendo in Josephite devotion [was] Pope John's decision to insert St. Joseph's name in the very center of the Church's prayer life, the Canon of the Mass."[1]

Pope Francis celebrated the 150th anniversary of Pope Leo XIII's declaration of St. Joseph as the Patron of the Universal Church with his Apostolic Letter "Patris corde." With the Letter, he proclaimed December 8, 2020 to December 8, 2021 as the Year of St. Joseph.

Just as two theologians, St. Augustine and St. Thomas Aquinas, laid the foundations for what became the edifice of Josephine theology, so also two Popes a hundred years apart issued encyclicals on St. Joseph that were definitive statements of the Church's teaching. The encyclicals were Leo XIII's *Quamquam Pluries* and John Paul II's *Redemptoris Custos*. The key doctrines and devotions associated with St. Joseph were henceforth no longer pious speculation but authoritative teaching.

The climax of the Church's response to St, Joseph is to be found in these two papal documents. It is wholly appropriate that we conclude our reflections with excerpts from these encyclicals that not only consolidate the insights of the past but break new ground.

QUAMQUAM PLURIES
ENCYCLICAL OF POPE LEO XIII
ON DEVOTION TO ST. JOSEPH
August 15th, 1889

The special motives for which St. Joseph has been proclaimed Patron of the Church, and from which the Church looks for singular benefit from his patronage and protection, are that Joseph was the spouse of Mary and that he was reputed the Father of Jesus Christ. From these sources have sprung his dignity, his holiness, his glory. In truth, the dignity of the Mother of God is so lofty that naught created can rank above it. But as Joseph has been united to the Blessed Virgin by the ties of marriage, it may not be doubted that he approached nearer than any to the eminent dignity by which the Mother of God surpasses so nobly all created natures. For marriage is the most intimate of all unions which from its essence imparts a community of gifts between those that by it are joined together. Thus in giving Joseph the Blessed Virgin as spouse, God appointed him to be not only her life's companion, the witness of her maidenhood, the protector of her honour, but also, by virtue of the conjugal tie, a participator in her sublime dignity....

And Joseph shines among all mankind by the most august dignity, since by divine will, he was the guardian of the Son of God and reputed as His father among men. Hence it came about that the Word of God was humbly subject to Joseph, that He obeyed him, and that He rendered to him all those offices that children are bound to render to their parents. From this two-fold dignity flowed the obligation which nature lays upon the head of families, so that Joseph became the guardian, the administrator, and the legal defender of the divine house whose chief he was. And during the whole course of his life he fulfilled those charges and those duties. He set himself to protect with a mighty love and a daily solicitude his spouse and the Divine Infant; regularly by his work he earned what was necessary for the one and the other for nourishment and clothing; he guarded from death the Child threatened by a monarch's jealousy, and found for Him a refuge; in the miseries of the journey and in the bitternesses of exile he was ever the companion, the assistance, and the upholder of the Virgin and of Jesus. Now the divine house which Joseph ruled with the authority of a father, contained within its limits the scarce-born Church. From the same fact that the most holy Virgin is the mother of Jesus Christ is she the mother of all Christians whom she bore on Mount Calvary amid the supreme throes of the Redemption; Jesus Christ is, in a manner, the first-born of Christians, who by the adoption and Redemption are his brothers. . And for such reasons the Blessed Patriarch looks upon the multitude of Christians who make up the Church as confided specially to his trust - this limitless family spread over the earth, over which, because he is the spouse of Mary and the Father of Jesus Christ he holds, as it were, a paternal authority. It is, then, natural and worthy that as the Blessed Joseph ministered to all the needs of the family at Nazareth and girt it about with his protection, he should now cover with the cloak of his heavenly patronage and defend the Church of Jesus Christ.....

And as the first [the Patriarch Joseph in the Old Testament] caused the prosperity of his master's domestic interests and at the same time rendered great services to the whole kingdom, so the second, destined to be the guardian of the Christian religion, should be regarded as the protector and defender of the Church, which is truly the house of the Lord and the kingdom of God on earth. These are the reasons why men of every rank and country should fly to the trust and guard of the blessed Joseph. Fathers of families find in Joseph the best personification of paternal solicitude and vigilance; spouses a perfect example of love, of peace, and of conjugal fidelity; virgins at the same time find in him the model and protector of virginal integrity. The noble of birth will earn of Joseph how to guard their dignity even in misfortune; the rich will understand, by his lessons, what are the goods most to be desired and won at the price of their labour. As to workmen, artisans, and persons of lesser degree, their recourse to Joseph is a special right, and his example is for their particular imitation. For Joseph, of royal blood, united by marriage to the greatest and holiest of women, reputed the father of the Son of God, passed his life in labour, and won by the toil of the artisan the needful support of his family. It is, then, true that the condition of the lowly has nothing shameful in it, and the work of the labourer is not only not dishonouring, but can, if virtue be joined to it, be singularly ennobled. Joseph, content with his slight possessions, bore the trials consequent on a fortune so slender, with greatness of soul, in imitation of his Son, who having put on the form of a slave, being the Lord of life, subjected himself of his own free-will to the spoliation and loss of everything.

APOSTOLIC EXHORTATION
REDEMPTORIS CUSTOS
OF THE SUPREME PONTIFF
JOHN PAUL II
ON THE PERSON AND MISSION OF
SAINT JOSEPH
IN THE LIFE OF CHRIST AND OF THE CHURCH
August 15, 1989

1. Inspired by the Gospel, the Fathers of the Church from the earliest centuries stressed that just as St. Joseph took loving care of Mary and gladly dedicated himself to Jesus Christ's upbringing,(1) he likewise watches over and protects Christ's Mystical Body,

that is, the Church, of which the Virgin Mary is the exemplar and model....

I gladly fulfill this pastoral duty so that all may grow in devotion to the Patron of the Universal Church and in love for the Savior whom he served in such an exemplary manner.

In this way the whole Christian people not only will turn to St. Joseph with greater fervor and invoke his patronage with trust, but also will always keep before their eyes his humble, mature way of serving and of "taking part" in the plan of salvation.(4)

I am convinced that by reflection upon the way that Mary's spouse shared in the divine mystery, the Church - on the road towards the future with all of humanity - will be enabled to discover ever anew her own identity within this redemptive plan, which is founded on the mystery of the Incarnation.

This is precisely the mystery in which Joseph of Nazareth "shared" like no other human being except Mary, the Mother of the Incarnate Word. He shared in it with her; he was involved in the same salvific event; he was the guardian of the same love, through the power of which the eternal Father "destined us to be his sons through Jesus Christ" (Eph 1:5).

5..... Together with Mary, Joseph is the first guardian of this divine mystery. Together with Mary, and in relation to Mary, he shares in this final phase of God's self-revelation in Christ and he does so from the very beginning. Looking at the gospel texts of both Matthew and Luke, one can also say that Joseph is the first to share in the faith of the Mother of God and that in doing so he supports his spouse in the faith of the divine annunciation. He is also the first to be placed by God on the path of Mary's "pilgrimage of faith." It is a path along which - especially at the time of Calvary and Pentecost - Mary will precede in a perfect way.(9)

6. The path that was Joseph's-his pilgrimage of faith - ended first, that is to say, before Mary stood at the foot of the cross on Golgotha, and before the time after Christ returned to the Father, when she was present in the upper room on Pentecost, the day the Church was manifested to the world, having been born in the power of the Spirit of truth. Nevertheless, Joseph's way of faith moved in the same direction: it was totally determined by the same mystery, of which he, together with Mary, had been the first guardian. The Incarnation and Redemption constitute an organic and indissoluble unity, in which "the plan of revelation is realized by words and deeds which are intrinsically bound up with each other."(10) Precisely because of this unity,

Pope John XXIII, who had a great devotion to St. Joseph, directed that Joseph's name be inserted in the Roman Canon of the Mass-which is the perpetual memorial of redemption - after the name of Mary and before the apostles, popes and martyrs.(11)

7. As can be deduced from the gospel texts, Joseph's marriage to Mary is the juridical basis of his fatherhood. It was to assure fatherly protection for Jesus that God chose Joseph to be Mary's spouse. It follows that Joseph's fatherhood - a relationship that places him as close as possible to Christ, to whom every election and predestination is ordered (cf. Rom 8:28-29) - comes to pass through marriage to Mary, that is, through the family....

Analyzing the nature of marriage, both St. Augustine and St. Thomas always identify it with an "indivisible union of souls," a "union of hearts," with "consent."(15) These elements are found in an exemplary manner in the marriage of Mary and Joseph. At the culmination of the history of salvation, when God reveals his love for humanity through the gift of the Word, it is precisely the marriage of Mary and Joseph that brings to realization in full "freedom" the "spousal gift of self" in receiving and expressing such a love.(16) "In this great undertaking which is the renewal of all things in Christ, marriage-it too purified and renewed-becomes a new reality, a sacrament of the New Covenant. We see that at the beginning of the New Testament, as at the beginning of the Old, there is a married couple. But whereas Adam and Eve were the source of evil which was unleashed on the world, Joseph and Mary arc the summit from which holiness spreads all over the earth. The Savior began the work of salvation by this virginal and holy union, wherein is manifested his all-powerful will to purify and sanctify the family - that sanctuary of love and cradle of life."(17)

How much the family of today can learn from this! "The essence and role of the family are in the final analysis specified by love. Hence the family has the mission to guard, reveal and communicate love, and this is a living reflection of and a real sharing in God's love for humanity and the love of Christ the Lord for the Church his bride."(18) This being the case, it is in the Holy Family, the original "Church in miniature (Ecclesia domestica),"(19) that every Christian family must be reflected. "Through God's mysterious design, it was in that family that the Son of God spent long years of a hidden life. It is therefore the prototype and example for all Christian families."(20)

8. St. Joseph was called by God to serve the person and mission of Jesus directly through the exercise

of his fatherhood. It is precisely in this way that, as the Church's Liturgy teaches, he "cooperated in the fullness of time in the great mystery of salvation" and is truly a "minister of salvation."(21) His fatherhood is expressed concretely "in his having made his life a service, a sacrifice to the mystery of the Incarnation and to the redemptive mission connected with it; in having used the legal authority which was his over the Holy Family in order to make a total gift of self, of his life and work; in having turned his human vocation to domestic love into a superhuman oblation of self, an oblation of his heart and all his abilities into love placed at the service of the Messiah growing up in his house."(22)

In recalling that "the beginnings of our redemption" were entrusted "to the faithful care of Joseph,"(23) the Liturgy specifies that "God placed him at the head of his family, as a faithful and prudent servant, so that with fatherly care he might watch over his only begotten Son."(24) Leo XIII emphasized the sublime nature of this mission: "He among all stands out in his august dignity, since by divine disposition he was guardian, and according to human opinion, father of God's Son. Whence it followed that the Word of God was subjected to Joseph, he obeyed him and rendered to him that honor and reverence that children owe to their father."(25)

Since it is inconceivable that such a sublime task would not be matched by the necessary qualities to adequately fulfill it, we must recognize that Joseph showed Jesus "by a special gift from heaven, all the natural love, all the affectionate solicitude that a father's heart can know."(26)

Besides fatherly authority over Jesus, God also gave Joseph a share in the corresponding love, the love that has its origin in the Father "from whom every family in heaven and on earth is named" (Eph 3:15).

The Gospels clearly describe the fatherly responsibility of Joseph toward Jesus. For salvation-which comes through the humanity of Jesus-is realized in actions which are an everyday part of family life, in keeping with that "condescension" which is inherent in the economy of the Incarnation. The gospel writers carefully show how in the life of Jesus nothing was left to chance, but how everything took place according to God's predetermined plan. The oft-repeated formula, "This happened, so that there might be fulfilled…," in reference to a particular event in the Old Testament serves to emphasize the unity and continuity of the plan which is fulfilled in Christ.

With the Incarnation, the "promises" and "figures" of the Old Testament become "reality": places, persons, events and rites interrelate according to precise divine commands communicated by angels and received by creatures who are particularly sensitive to the voice of God. Mary is the Lord's humble servant, prepared from eternity for the task of being the Mother of God. Joseph is the one whom God chose to be the "overseer of the Lord's birth,"(27) the one who has the responsibility to look after the Son of God's "ordained" entry into the world, in accordance with divine dispositions and human laws. All of the so-called "private" or "hidden" life of Jesus is entrusted to Joseph's guardianship.

20..... On the other hand, it was from his marriage to Mary that Joseph derived his singular dignity and his rights in regard to Jesus. "It is certain that the dignity of the Mother of God is so exalted that nothing could be more sublime; yet because Mary was united to Joseph by the bond of marriage, there can be no doubt but that Joseph approached as no other person ever could that eminent dignity whereby the Mother of God towers above all creatures. Since marriage is the highest degree of association and friendship involving by its very nature a communion of goods, it follows that God, by giving Joseph to the Virgin, did not give him to her only as a companion for life, a witness of her virginity and protector of her honor: he also gave Joseph to Mary in order that he might share, through the marriage pact, in her own sublime greatness."(33)

21. This bond of charity was the core of the Holy Family's life, first in the poverty of Bethlehem, then in their exile in Egypt, and later in the house of Nazareth. The Church deeply venerates this Family, and proposes it as the model of all families. Inserted directly in the mystery of the Incarnation, the Family of Nazareth has its own special mystery. And in this mystery, as in the Incarnation, one finds a true fatherhood: the human form of the family of the Son of God, a true human family, formed by the divine mystery. In this family, Joseph is the father: his fatherhood is not one that derives from begetting offspring; but neither is it an "apparent" or merely "substitute" fatherhood. Rather, it is one that fully shares in authentic human fatherhood and the mission of a father in the family. This is a consequence of the hypostatic union: humanity taken up into the unity of the Divine Person of the Word-Son, Jesus Christ. Together with human nature, all that is human, and especially the family - as the first dimension of man's existence in the world - is also taken up in Christ. Within this context, Joseph's human fatherhood was also "taken up" in the mystery of Christ's Incarnation.

On the basis of this principle, the words which Mary spoke to the twelve-year-old Jesus in the Temple take on their full significance: "Your father and I... have been looking for you." This is no conventional phrase: Mary's words to Jesus show the complete reality of the Incarnation present in the mystery of the Family of Nazareth. From the beginning, Joseph accepted with the "obedience of faith" his human fatherhood over Jesus. And thus, following the light of the Holy Spirit who gives himself to human beings through faith, he certainly came to discover ever more fully the indescribable gift that was his human fatherhood.

27. The communion of life between Joseph and Jesus leads us to consider once again the mystery of the Incarnation, precisely in reference to the humanity of Jesus as the efficacious instrument of his divinity for the purpose of sanctifying man: "By virtue of his divinity, Christ's human actions were salvific for us, causing grace within us, either by merit or by a certain efficacy."(39)

Among those actions, the gospel writers highlight those which have to do with the Paschal Mystery, but they also underscore the importance of physical contact with Jesus for healing (cf. for example, Mk 1:41), and the influence Jesus exercised upon John the Baptist when they were both in their mothers' wombs (cf. Lk 1:41-44).

As we have seen, the apostolic witness did not neglect the story of Jesus' birth, his circumcision, his presentation in the Temple, his flight into Egypt and his hidden life in Nazareth. It recognized the "mystery" of grace present in each of these saving "acts," inasmuch as they all share the same source of love: the divinity of Christ. If through Christ's humanity this love shone on all mankind, the first beneficiaries were undoubtedly those whom the divine will had most intimately associated with itself: Mary, the Mother of Jesus, and Joseph, his presumed father.(40)

Why should the "fatherly" love of Joseph not have had an influence upon the "filial" love of Jesus? And vice versa why should the "filial" love of Jesus not have had an influence upon the "fatherly" love of Joseph, thus leading to a further deepening of their unique relationship? Those souls most sensitive to the impulses of divine love have rightly seen in Joseph a brilliant example of the interior life.…

28. At a difficult time in the Church's history, Pope Pius IX, wishing to place her under the powerful patronage of the holy patriarch Joseph, declared him "Patron of the Catholic Church."(42) For

Pius IX this was no idle gesture, since by virtue of the sublime dignity which God has granted to his most faithful servant Joseph, "the Church, after the Blessed Virgin, his spouse, has always held him in great honor and showered him with praise, having recourse to him amid tribulations."(43)

What are the reasons for such great confidence? Leo XIII explained it in this way: "The reasons why St. Joseph must be considered the special patron of the Church, and the Church in turn draws exceeding hope from his care and patronage, chiefly arise from his having been the husband of Mary and the presumed father of Jesus..., Joseph was in his day the lawful and natural guardian, head and defender of the Holy Family.... It is thus fitting and most worthy of Joseph's dignity that, in the same way that he once kept unceasing holy watch over the family of Nazareth, so now does he protect and defend with his heavenly patronage the Church of Christ."(44)

29. This patronage must be invoked as ever necessary for the Church, not only as a defense against all dangers, but also, and indeed primarily, as an impetus for her renewed commitment to evangelization in the world and to re-evangelization in those lands and nations where-as I wrote in the Apostolic Exhortation *Christideles Laici* - "religion and the Christian life were formerly flourishing

and…are now put to a hard test."(45) In order to bring the first proclamation of Christ, or to bring it anew wherever it has been neglected or forgotten, the Church has need of special "power from on high" (cf. Lk 24:49; Acts 1:8): a gift of the Spirit of the Lord, a gift which is not unrelated to the intercession and example of his saints.

30. Besides trusting in Joseph's sure protection, the Church also trusts in his noble example, which transcends all individual states of life and serves as a model for the entire Christian community, whatever the condition and duties of each of its members may be.…

Already at the beginning of human redemption, after Mary, we find the model of obedience made incarnate in St. Joseph, the man known for having faithfully carried out God's commands.

Pope Paul VI invited us to invoke Joseph's patronage "as the Church has been wont to do in these recent times, for herself in the first place, with a spontaneous theological reflection on the marriage of divine and human action in the great economy of the Redemption, in which economy the first-the divine one-is wholly sufficient unto itself, while the second-the human action which is ours-though capable of nothing (cf. Jn 15:5), is never dispensed from a humble but conditional and ennobling collaboration. The Church also calls upon Joseph as her protector because of a profound and ever present desire to reinvigorate her ancient life with true evangelical virtues, such as shine forth in St. Joseph."(47)

31.… One hundred years ago, Pope Leo XIII had already exhorted the Catholic world to pray for the protection of St. Joseph, Patron of the whole Church. The Encyclical Epistle *Quamquam Pluries* appealed to Joseph's "fatherly love…for the child Jesus" and commended to him, as "the provident guardian of the divine Family," "the beloved inheritance which Jesus Christ purchased by his blood." Since that time-as I recalled at the beginning of this Exhortation-the Church has implored the protection of St. Joseph on the basis of "that sacred bond of charity which united him to the Immaculate Virgin Mother of God," and the Church has commended to Joseph all of her cares, including those dangers which threaten the human family.

Even today we have many reasons to pray in a similar way: "Most beloved father, dispel the evil of falsehood and sin…graciously assist us from heaven in our struggle with the powers of darkness…and just as once you saved the Child Jesus from mortal danger, so now defend God's holy Church from the snares of her enemies and from all adversity."(49) Today we still have good reason to commend everyone to St. Joseph.

May St. Joseph obtain for the Church and for the world, as well as for each of us, the blessing of the Father, Son and Holy Spirit.

Application

Findings are followed by their applications. The finding of the quantum world led to the creation of a whole host of technologies. The self-revelation of Jesus was the greatest possible disclosure in history because it changed our whole understanding of God and humanity and has an immediate urgent application to our own lives. The recognition of his mother was part of this application to our lives as is the recognition now of his virginal father. Both Mary and Joseph are gifts given to us by Jesus. And both are integral parts of his plan of salvation for the human race. Together the three of them constitute the Holy Family which we are now invited to join. To fully accept Jesus is to accept his family for father and mother help us in growing in our love for their Son, our brother. In this third millennium of Christianity, the world is invited to "find" the head of the Holy Family who is appointed the protector of all who belong to the Family of Jesus.

The logical and theological sequel to the "finding" of St. Joseph is the Holy Family. The "Holy Family" is the fullest "application" of what we have learned about St. Joseph. And so we turn next to this application in the sequel.

NOTES

In the Fullness of Time

[1] Fr. Stanley Smolenski was one of the first to write about "St. Joseph's place in the third millennium." Mark Drogin has pointedly insisted that we cannot see Jesus in isolation from his family

The Seven Signs

[1] Cf. F. L. Filas, S.J., joseph: The Man Closest to jesus (Boston: St. Paul Editions, 1962), 462. https://traditioninaction.org/HotTopics/f163_Dialogue_80.htm

[2] "Remarques sur la Constitution dogmatique sur l'Église 'Lumen gentium'," *Irénikon* 1(1966) 5-45 at 22-24.)

Heaven has spoken –
Encounters of the Third Order

[1] http://catholicsaints.mobi/ebooks/amk/amk.htm

[2] https://www.piercedhearts.org/treasures/shrines/joseph_knock.htm

[3] Ibid.

[4] https://www.catholiccompany.com/getfed/apparition-st-joseph-at-fatima-6027

[5] https://www.zeitun-eg.org/zeitoun1.htm

[6] https://indefenseofthecross.com/marian-apparitions/our-lady-of-zeitoun-egypt/

[7] https://icxcmary.wordpress.com/akita-japan/

[8] http://bit.ly/2DCSXoY

[9] https://www.piercedhearts.org/hearts_jesus_mary/apparitions/akita.html#Messages

[10] Teiji Yasuda, O.S.V., *The Tears and Message of Mary* (Asbury, New Jersey: 1989), 167.

[11] Thomas W. Petrisko, *St. Joseph and the Triumph of the Saints* (McKees Rock, PA: St. Andrews, 1998), 204.

[12] http://bit.ly/2pjvaoU

[13] Petrisko, *The Fatima Prophecies* (McKees Rock, PA: St. Andrews, 1998), 4.

[14] Ibid., 5.

[15] Petrisko, *St. Joseph and the Triumph of the Saints*, op cit., 198.

[16] Ibid., 196.

[17] John Haffert, *To Prevent This* (Asbury, NJ: The 101 Foundation, 1993), 50.

[18] Joseph F. Chorpenning, "The Historical Development of the Holy Family Devotion" in Michael D. Griffin ed. *Saint Joseph and the Third Millennium* (Hubertus, Wisconsin: Teresian Charism Press, 1999), 187-88, 191.

Dreamer and Doer – the Biblical Story

[1] Richard Foley, *St. Joseph – Patron of the Triumph* (Goleta, CA: Queenship, 2002), 16.

[2] Joseph T. Lienhard, *St. Joseph in Early Christianity* (Philadelphia, PA: Saint Joseph's University Press, 1999), 21, 24.

[3] Ibid., 24-6

⁴John Paul II, *Guardian of the Redeemer* (Santa Cruz, CA: Guardian of the Redeemer Books, 2000), 22.

⁵Lucien Deiss, *Joseph, Mary, Jesus* (Collegeville, MN: Liturgical Press, 1996), 6-7.

⁶Larry M. Toschi in "Saint Joseph in Sacred Scripture" in Michael D. Griffin ed. *Saint Joseph and the Third Millennium* (Hubertus, Wisconsin: Teresian Charism Press, 1999), 50-1.

⁷https://www.catholic.com/magazine/print-edition/was-jesus-an-only-child

⁸http://osjusa.org/st-joseph/scripture/joseph-in-the-gospel-of-luke/ii-2-joseph-son-of-adam-son-of-david/

⁹Larry M. Toschi, *Joseph in the New Testament* (Santa Cruz, CA: Guardian of the Redeemer Books, 1991, 93-7.

¹⁰Jerome cited in Joseph T. Lienhard, *St. Joseph in Early Christianity*, op cit., 42.

¹¹https://www.catholicculture.org/culture/library/view.cfm?recnum=9298

¹²Commentarius in epistolam ad Galatas, lectio 5; Opera 21, 185: "Si Dominus matrem virginem noluit nisi virgini commendare custodiendam,

quomodo sustinuisset sponsum ejus virginem non fuisse et sic perstitisse?"

[13] Larry M. Toschi, *Joseph in the New Testament*, op cit., 27-33.

[14] http://campus.udayton.edu/mary/Rossier.html

[15] H.E. iii:32. Cited in Harold Riley, "The Brothers of the Lord," *Downside Review*, January 1998..

[16] bid., H.E. iii:20.

[17] Gordon Wakefield, "The Methodist Point of View," in **Mother of Jesus** (London: Ecumenical Society for the Blessed Virgin Mary, 1968), 8.

[18] "The Brothers of Jesus and His Mother's Virginity," *The Thomist* 63, 1999.

[19] Weimer's *The Works of Luther*, English translation by Pelikan, Concordia, St. Louis, v. 11, pp. 319-320; v. 6. p. 510.

[20] Bernard Leeming, "Protestants and Our Lady," Marian Library Studies, January 1967, p. 9.

[21] *Zwingli Opera, Corpus Reformatorum*, Berlin, 1905, v. 1, p. 424.)

[22] David F. Wright, ed., *Chosen by God: Mary in Evangelical Perspective* (London: Marshall Pickering, 1989), 170-1.

[23] Jerome cited in Joseph T. Lienhard, *St. Joseph in Early Christianity*, op cit., 41-2.

[24] Introduction to the revised and expanded edition. Richard Burridge, *What Are the Gospels? A Comparison with Greco-Roman Biography* (Grand Rapids: Eerdmans, 2004), viii-ix.

[25] Christopher Tuckett, *From the Sayings to the Gospels* (Tubingen, Germany: Mohr Siebeck, 2014), 116.

[26] William Farmer, The Gospel of Jesus (Louisville, KY: Westminster John Knox Press, 1994), 160.

[27] Ibid., 130.

[28] Richard Burridge, *What Are The Gospels? A Comparison With Graeco-Roman Biography* (Cambridge: Cambridge University Press, 1992), 194-195.

[29] Ben Witherington in Joel B. Green, et al., editors, *Dictionary of Jesus and the Gospels* (Downers Grove, Illinois: InterVarsity Press, 1992), 61.

[30] Robert Karris, in Raymond Brown, et al., editors, *The New Jerome Biblical Commentary* (Englewood Cliffs, New Jersey: Prentice Hall, 1990), 679.

[31] Howard W. Clarke, *The Gospel of Matthew and Its Readers: A Historical Introduction to the First Gospel* (Bloomington, IN: Indiana University Press, 2003), 9.

[32]"Christianity and Paganism" in http://www.bede.org.uk/frazer.htm.

[33]Craig. S. Keener, "Matt 1.18," *The Bible Background Commentary*, (Downers Grove, Illinois: InterVarsity Press, 1993).

[34]"Birth of Jesus," *Dictionary of Jesus and the Gospels*, Joel Green, Scot McKnight, I Howard Marshall (eds.), (Downers Grove, Illinois: InterVarsity Press, 1992).

[35]Craig Keener, *Commentary on Matthew* (Downers Grove, Illinois: InterVarsity Press, 1997) 25, 47.

[36]*Matthew* (Grand Rapids, Michigan: InterVarsity Press, 1999), 71.

The Testimony of "Tradition"

[1]Joseph T. Lienhard, *St. Joseph in Early Christianity* (Philadelphia, PA: Saint Joseph's University Press, 1999), 18.

[2]Ibid, 50ff.

[3]Ibid, 27.

[4]Leon Christiani (Derby, N.Y.: St. Paul Publications, 1967), 85.

[5]http://www.newadvent.org/fathers/0805.htm.

[6] Michael Griffin, *Saint Joseph – A Theological Introduction* (Montreal, Canada: Oratoire Saint-Joseph, 1972), 7.

[7] Joseph T. Lienhard, op cit., 28.

The Saints' Saint

[1] Hom. 2 super Missus est, 11.16: PL 183, 69-70.

[2] http://www.piercedhearts.org/theology_heart/teaching_saints/a_teaching_saints.htm

[3] *The Autobiography of St. Teresa*, chapter 6.

[4] St. Francis of Sales: Discourse 19 in Complete Works of St. Francis of Sales, VI.

[5] https://richardconlin.wordpress.com/2015/03/19/st-joseph/

Theological Momentum

[1] https://www.catholicculture.org/culture/library/view.cfm?recnum=7532

[2] http://www.thesumma.info/saviour/saviour77.php

[3] Michael Griffin, *Saint Joseph – A Theological Introduction* (Montreal, Canada: Oratoire Saint-Joseph, 1972), 8-9.

[4] Ibid., 12.

[5] Ibid., 28-30.

[6] John Calvin, *Institutes of the Christian Religion*, Volume II (Philadelphia: Presbyterian Board of Christian Education).

[7] Citation in John Murray, *Calvin on Scripture and Divine Sovereignty* (Michigan: Baker Book House, 1960), 61.

[8] Martin Luther, *Bondage of the Will*, translated J.I. Packer and O.R. Johnston (Revell: 1957), 217.

[9] John Wesley, "Predestination Calmly Considered," in Albert C. Outler, ed. *John Wesley* (New York: Oxford University Press, 1964), 451.

[10] John MacQuarrie, *Mary for All Christians* (London: T&T Clark, 2001), 104.

[11] H. Edward Symonds, "The Blessed Virgin Mary," in *The Blessed Virgin Mary: Essays by Anglican Writers*, E.L. Mascall and H.S. Box, eds. (London: Darton, Longman & Todd Ltd, 1963), 6-7.

Devotional Crescendo

[1] http://anglicanexfide.blogspot.com/2010/03/coptic-devotion-to-s-joseph.html

[2] Edward Healy Thompson, The life and glories of St. Joseph (London: Burns and Oates, 1888), 449-451.

[3] http://osjusa.org/st-joseph/liturgy/part-a/

[4] Ibid.

[5] Ibid.

[6] Ibid.

[7] Agenzia Fides 18/03/2010, http://www.fides.org/aree/news/newsdet.php?idnews=26305&lan=eng

The Church Says "Yes"

[1] https://stjsa.org/the-pope-of-st-joseph

The Once and Future Family
Jesus, Mary and Joseph

Contents

Discovery Channel 213

The Gospel Code – *the Holy Family–Holy Trinity Nexus* 226

Mapping the Earthly and Heavenly Families..245

Entering the Family of God 255

All in the Family 271

"The simple mention of Jesus, Mary and Joseph reminds us that there [in the Holy Family] **we find all human history** and there we find also the salvation, the grandeur, the beauty, the splendor of the Catholic Church." Pope John XXIII. Address to the street-cleaners of Rome, March 19,1961.

"In this great undertaking which is the renewal of all things in Christ, marriage—it too purified and renewed—becomes a new reality, a sacrament of the New Covenant. We see that at the beginning of the New Testament, as at the beginning of the Old, there is a married couple. But whereas Adam and Eve were the source of evil which was unleashed on the world, Joseph and Mary are the summit from which holiness spreads all over the earth. The Savior began the work of salvation by this virginal and holy union, wherein is manifested his all-powerful will to purify and sanctify the family—that sanctuary of love and cradle of life." Pope Paul VI, Discourse to the Equipes Notre Dame Movement, May 4, 1970

"At the culmination of the history of salvation, when God reveals his love for humanity through the gift of the Word, it is precisely the marriage of Mary and Joseph that brings to realization in full "freedom" the "spousal gift of self" in receiving and expressing such a love. (#7) … The apostolic witness did not neglect the story of Jesus' birth, his circumcision, his presentation in the Temple, his flight into Egypt and his hidden life in Nazareth. It recognized the "mystery" of grace present in each of these saving "acts," inasmuch as they all share the same source of love: the divinity of Christ. If through Christ's humanity this love shone on all mankind, the first beneficiaries were undoubtedly those whom the divine will had most intimately associated with itself: Mary, the Mother of Jesus, and Joseph, his presumed father. (#27) ... This bond of charity was the core of the Holy Family's life, first in the poverty of Bethlehem, then in their exile in Egypt, and later in the house of Nazareth. The Church deeply venerates this Family, and proposes it as the model of all families. Inserted directly in the mystery of the Incarnation, the Family of Nazareth has its own special mystery. And in this mystery, as in the Incarnation, one finds a true fatherhood: the human form of the family of the Son of God, a true human family, formed by the divine mystery. (#21) ... It is in the Holy Family, the original "Church in miniature (Ecclesia domestica),"[19] that every Christian family must be reflected. "Through God's mysterious design, it was in that family that the Son of God spent long years of a hidden life. It is therefore the prototype and example for all Christian families." (#7). Pope John Paul II, *Redemptoris Custos*

"The Holy Family of Nazareth, the harmonious reflection on earth of the life of the Most Holy Trinity." Pope Benedict XVI, Message for the 49th World Day of Prayer for Vocations, April 29 2012.

The discovery of Joseph led inescapably and immediately to the discovery of the Holy Family, the First Family of redeemed humanity. In this we see an intellectual and spiritual journey that came to a climax in the pontificate of Leo XIII who, in 1892, published the apostolic brief *Neminem Fugit* described as "the *magna carta* of the Holy Family devotion in modern times" and then, in 1893, instituted the liturgical Feast of the Holy Family.

Prior to *Neminem Fugit* and his addition of the Holy Family Feast into the Church calendar, Leo, in 1890, had approved the Association of Christian Families Consecrated to the Holy Family and the formula of consecration of Christian families before the Holy Family. This was the same Leo who had published the landmark encyclical on St. Joseph.

At any rate, once Joseph was discovered to be truly the husband of Mary and truly the father of Jesus, it was possible to deconstruct the ancient apocryphal cul de sacs and return to the story plainly laid out in Sacred Scripture: Jesus belonged to a family of father, mother and child and God's plan of redemption was realized through this family. Jesus, of course, is the Source and Center of redemption but as "a consequence of the hypostatic union," in John Paul's words, "humanity [is] taken up into the unity of the Divine Person of the Word-Son, Jesus Christ. Together with human nature, *all that is human, and especially the family*—as the first dimension of man's existence in the world—is also taken up in Christ." (Redemptoris Custos #21). This is true first and foremost in the Holy Family for here, he says, we find "the human form of the family of the Son of God, a true human family, formed by the divine mystery

The Holy Family is a mystical reality in its own right. It is a reality that is a relationship. "Historians of spirituality maintain that devotion to the Holy Family truly comes into its own when Jesus, Mary and Joseph are reflected upon not individually but in relationship to one another. This is precisely the perspective of Francis [de Sales], who focuses on the Holy Family's triple bond of love: the spousal love of Mary and Joseph, the filial and paternal love of Jesus and Joseph, and the filial and maternal love of Jesus and Mary." This triple bond is not only a "model" for all other families but all persons and families are invited to become part of the Holy Family. Divinization came to the human race through the

Divinizer who was himself the child of a divinized couple ("Hail full of grace," "Joseph was a just man").

Like all discoveries, scientific and theological, the recognition of the Holy Family transforms our perspectives and plans. Nothing can be the same for those who come to see this dimension of God's redemptive plan: it all begins with a family, a family that reflects God's own Triune reality, a family that is active through all of salvation history, a family that we are called to enter through consecration, a family that is FOREVER.

As has been said, the significance of the family of Jesus should (in hindsight!) have been intuitively obvious to Christians right from the start. To be saved, you have to become a brother or sister of Jesus whose humanity "connects" us to his divinity. But Jesus is "related" to the human race only because of and through his family: he receives his human nature from his Mother and his human identity cannot be disengaged from his parentage: "Is he not the carpenter's son? Is not his mother named Mary?" (Matthew 13:55). To become a brother or sister of Jesus is to become a son or daughter of Joseph and Mary.

Discovery Channel

The "finding" of the Holy Family followed an intuitively coherent sequence. Only if we understand the identity and role of Joseph can we appreciate the significance of his family. Given that this discovery took nearly twenty centuries (!), it would be understandable that a further breakthrough would be more recent in provenance. Surprisingly, however, the early stages in the discovery of the Holy Family almost parallel the first stages of the discovery of Joseph going as far back as the 14th century with Jean Gerson (1363-1429), the main theologian of the Council of Constance.

But there was another unique obstacle to recognizing the Holy Family: it was the need to discover the family(!) which was really a problem of concepts and terms. "The absence of reference to the family of Nazareth as a group was due mainly to the fact that, until around the beginning of the seventeenth century, the idea of family was much wider than the way we think of it today – father, mother and children. The word 'family' was used in the sense of 'household' and referred to all the people under the authority of the head of the house, including relatives and servants. It could also be used to mean the servants alone.... The emergence of the theme of Jesus, Mary and Joseph as a family group, in late sixteenth and seventeenth-century spirituality - as well as being due to the change in the meaning of the word 'family' - resulted, for the most part, from the development of an interest in and devotion to St Joseph."[1]

Once the true portrait of St. Joseph was restored, his connection to his family was seen in a new light – as a normal family albeit one engaged in the most important mission in human history. Gerson himself, known for his work on St. Joseph, began the exploration of the Holy Family: 'a mystery so profound and hidden for centuries, this trinity so worthy of wonder and veneration, Jesus, Joseph and Mary.'[2] "Gerson's transformation of St. Joseph's image made it possible to think about the Holy Family in a new way. Gerson also made it possible to speak about the Holy Family by coining the expression 'earthly trinity' to speak about Jesus, Mary and Joseph as a nuclear family in the modern sense. Although Gerson did not explicitly compare the earthly trinity of Jesus, Mary and Joseph with the blessed Trinity in heaven, such a comparison is implicit since previously the use of the word was reserved to the three divine Persons. Henceforth, it became popular to refer to and to depict in the visual arts the Holy Family as a trinity which replicated on earth the blessed Trinity in heaven."[3]

These were years when the family was under tremendous stress from both external threats such as famines, plagues and wars but also internal pressures caused by marked age gaps between husbands and wives and alienated offspring. Gerson, and after him, St. Bernardine of Siena (1380-1444) offered the Holy Family as the role model for the family: "The wise assiduous, and diligent household head could partially ward off the social, political, and economic evils menacing the family just as St. Joseph rescued the Christ Child and the Virgin Mary from the murderous Herod, supported them in Egypt by his trade as carpenter, and protected them on their perilous journeys. Devotion to St. Joseph and to the Holy Family was viewed as particularly well suited to those entering the married state and thus assuming the grace responsibilities of directing a household. The Holy Family's affective life also spoke to the family's internal crisis of affection." St. Joseph "was not only an effective manager, he was also a loving father. Joseph was bound to Mary and Jesus, and they to him, by bonds of deep affection. Gerson expresses it this way …: "Oh, venerable trinity Jesus, Joseph and Mary, which divinity has joined, the concor of love.' 'The concord of love': this is the cultural and emotional ideal to which late medieval families were invited to aspire."[4] The Holy

Family served also as a model for religious orders of mendicants who took a vow of poverty.

Shortly after Gerson, the Spanish Franciscan Francisco de Osuna (1492-1540) blazed a new trail by further exploring the parallelism between the earthly trinity of Jesus, Mary and Joseph and the Holy Trinity. Such explorations continued with later writers. St Teresa of Avila (1515-1582), inspired by a private revelation, introduced yet another dimension by encouraging believers to become a part of the Holy Family. This was indeed the driving force of her renewal of Carmel: "prior to its foundation, the saint has another vision, in which God defines what He wishes the world of the first reformed Carmel to be: the world of the Holy Family, a 'little dwelling corner' and 'abode' for Jesus watched over by Mary and Joseph … 'One day after Communion, His Majesty earnestly commanded me to strive for this new monastery with all my powers … He said it should be called St. Joseph and that this saint would keep watch over us at one door, and our Lay at the other, that Christ would remain with us.'"[5] As Teresa saw it, the relationship with the Holy Family should be personal for all believers: "Teresa is one of those rare individuals in Christian history who has a profound consciousness of the inseparability and integrity of Jesus, Mary, and Joseph.… It has been observed that

Teresa rediscovered 'the incarnation of the Infant Jesus, of Mary, of Joseph, as living human beings, with whom one could speak on familiar terms, who answered you, who were interested in you.'"[6]

St. Francis de Sales (1567-1622) was another great apostle of the Holy Family. He taught that the Holy Family was the model for marriage, family and religious communities. Like St. Teresa he entered into a personal relationship with Jesus, Mary and Joseph. "In his biography of 'Holy Charity,' his magisterial *Treatise on the Love of God* (1616), addressed to 'any human heart anxious to grow in the love of God,' Francis esteems the Holy Family as the example par excellence of magnanimous love. Complementing his dedication of the *Introduction* to Jesus, the 'divine Child,' Francis dedicates the *Treatise* 'to the mother of charity and to the father of heartfelt love,' the Virgin Mary and St. Joseph. For Francis, Mary and Joseph are a 'pair without peer,' because they excelled in magnanimous love by the service they rendered 'that divine Child who is the Savior of those who love and the love of those saved,' their beloved Jesus, 'king of all hearts, whom [their] hearts adore.' In the *Treatise*, Francis presents a profound meditation on the bond of love that unites Jesus, Mary, and Joseph. This meditation reflects three key themes of Francis' doctrine of marriage and family life – the union of hearts as the essence of marriage, the responsibility of both parents for raising children and the filial devotion owed parents – thereby implicitly proffering the Holy Family as a model for families."[7]

Francis underlines the scriptural and theological foundations for devotion to the Holy Family: "Without the marriage of Mary and Joseph, there would be no Holy Family. According to Francis, the bond of love that binds the members of the Holy Family is a union of hearts which comes about through the marriage of Mary and Joseph. Mary and Jesus were so completely united with one another that they 'had but one soul, but one heart, and but one life, so that the Blessed Mother, although living, yet did not live herself but rather the Son lived in her.' And through the indissoluble union that Jesus establishes between Joseph's heart and Mary's heart, He draws the saint into union with His own divine heart. Jesus was 'the dear Child of [Joseph's] heart,' and Joseph was Jesus' 'great friend and His beloved father.' … The rich affective language in which Francis casts his statements about the spousal and parental love of Mary and Joseph and Jesus' filial love exalts the Holy Family as the paradigm of the mutual affection and support that is to be hallmark of married and family life…. Francis held that from his marriage to the Virgin Mary, Joseph derived his singular dignity and his rights in regard to Jesus.

Within the divine plan, this marriage was ordained to provide a human family for the Son of God, to receive and to rear Jesus Christ. Joseph was thus chosen 'to perform the most tender and loving duties that ever were or ever shall be done in behalf of the Son of God, with the exception of those done by his heavenly Spouse, the true natural Mother of that same Son.' ... For Francis, as for St. Teresa, the members of the Holy Family are inseparable. He cannot look at one without thinking of the others: 'Mother all triumphant, who can cast his eyes on you in majesty without seeing at your right hand him whom your Son, out of love for you, willed so often to honor with the title of father.'"[8]

The Holy Family, in fact, represents the Holy Trinity. This Family is "a trinity on earth representing in some sort the most holy Trinity. Mary, Jesus, and Joseph – Joseph, Jesus, and Mary – a trinity worthy indeed to be honored and greatly esteemed."[9] As we shall see, this rich insight opens the door to a whole host of scriptural insights

Another pioneer was Jean Jacques Olier (1608-1657) also known for his attachment to the Holy House of Loreto. "The connection between the Holy Family and Loreto is that according to an ancient tradition, the house contained in the shrine at Loreto in the north of Italy, is the one where Our Lady lived with her parents and where the Annunciation took place. It was also popularly believed that the Holy Family lived there from the time they returned from their exile in Egypt as Anna and Joachim, Our Lady's parents, had died by then. The house is reputed to have been brought by angels (some say it was brought stone by stone by the Crusaders; others say by a family called de Angelis) from Nazareth, first to Illyrium in 1291 and then to Loreto in 1294. Olier went on pilgrimage to Loreto in 1630 and experienced both physical and spiritual healing there."[10]

The devotion spread across Europe. The Cistercian Bernard Rosa (1624-1696) from Silesia in Poland described Jesus, Mary and Joseph as "'the created Trinity,' 'the Church in its embryonic state' and 'the first living Church.' He saw Jesus, Mary and Joseph together as being 'great in love, united in love, and helping the faithful in all their needs.' In his writing he demonstrated how Jesus, Mary and Joseph are the powerful protectors of the Church in its struggle to gain the respect due to the name of God since the death of Jesus Christ. Rosa also published several prayers in honour of St. Joseph where the three members of the Holy Family are seen together. He saw imitation of the lives of St Joseph and of the Holy Family as one of the most important Christian duties."[11]

St. Alphonsus Ligouri (1696-1787) called the Holy Family "the earthly Trinitarian family."

One remarkable dimension of the devotion of the Holy Family was its immediate influence in the New World. This devotion was part and parcel of the very introduction of Christianity in New Spain (Canada, Mexico and the Philippines) and New France (from Canada to the Gulf of Mexico) in the sixteenth and seventeenth centuries. "In New Spain, the parents of Jesus also became the parents of the Amerindians. For example, as the earthly father of Jesus, St. Joseph was not only a role model for the Amerindians, he also became *their* father.… The Virgin Mary became their loving and compassionate mother, while Joseph, who rescued the Christ Child from the murderous Herod, became the father of this conquered and oppressed people who would protect and shelter them."[12]

New France went further than New Spain in fostering liturgical devotion to the Holy Family.

> "New France would anticipate by more than two centuries the Universal Church's adoption of the Feast of the Holy Family. The impetus for this initiative in New France was the strong devotion to the Holy Family that flourished among the first colonists." 47 A French Ursuline

nun, Blessed Marie of the Incarnation (1599-1672) reported that she was commanded by God "to build a house in Canada in which He would be adored and praised in company with Jesus and Mary ... along with St. Joseph who should never be separated from them."48. Marie arrived in Quebec on August 1 1639, the Feast of the Espousal of the Virgin Mary and St. Joseph. The Holy Family played a central role in the constitution they adopted for their work. The founding of the city of Montreal is particularly linked to the Holy Family devotion. The settlement of the city was organized by Fr. Jean Jacques Olier (1608-1657), the founder of the Sulpicians, and a layman Jérôme le Royer de la Dauversière (1597 – 1659). Both were devotees of the Holy Family and Dauversière, in fact, had a vision of the Holy Family. In 1642, they and their partners in France "consecrated the island of Montreal to the Holy Family of Our Lord, Jesus, Mary and Joseph, under the special protection of the Blessed Virgin."51). Fr. Pierre Joseph Marie Chaumonot (1611-1693) "was instrumental in the foundation, first at Montreal and then at Quebec, of confraternities of the Holy Family, the purpose of which was 'the sanctification of Christian families, on the model of the [family] of the Word incarnate.'"[13]

Blessed Francois-Xavier de Montmorency-Laval, the first bishop of Quebec (1674-85) further fostered devotion to the Holy Family. On November 14, 1684, Bishop Laval instituted the first ever feast of the Holy Family in a diocese, his diocese of Quebec – 237 years before it became a feast of the Church as a whole.[14]

It was Pope Leo XIII (1878-1903) who formally introduced the theology of the Holy Family to the universal Church. In the 19th century the institution of the family was threatened by the Industrial Revolution and the State. Leo's response was *Rerum Novarum*. In this encyclical he points out that the family is "anterior to every kind of State or nation, with rights and duties of its own, totally independent of the commonwealth."[15] Along with his concern for the integrity of the family, Leo, as we have noted, promoted devotion to the Holy Family with his institution of the Feast of the Holy Family, his approval of the Holy Family confraternity and his apostolic brief on the devotion.

In *Neminem Fugit*, Leo showed why the Holy Family should be the model for every family:

> Therefore, by divine disposition of Providence, it [the Holy Family] appeared to be structured in a way that every Christian, whatever one's

state and situation in life, might, through contemplation, readily find in it inspiration and incentive for the practice of all the virtues. Hence, Joseph is the outstanding model of paternal care and concern for fathers; for mothers, Mary, the Mother of God, is the sublime ideal of love, modesty, obedience and perfect fidelity; and for the children, Jesus, the Son of God, subject to Mary and to Joseph, is the divine model of loving obedience to be admired, honored, and imitated.

All persons of sound upbringing will learn from this Family of royal lineage how to be disciplined in prosperity and dignified in adversity: and the rich to prefer virtues to riches. Workers as well as those who, particularly in our own time, suffer so bitterly because of the poor and difficult family condition, will be able to experience, in spite of the situation in which they find themselves, joy rather than affliction if they seriously reflect upon the poor and simple lifestyle of that Holy Family. Their efforts and concerns for their own daily existence are the same as those of God's own human family: for Joseph had to provide for the family needs from his own work, and even Jesus' own divine hands became hardened by manual labor.

Subsequent to Leo's papacy, over a hundred religious communities, associations and institutes under the patronage of the Holy Family sprang up across the world. After Leo, Pope Benedict XV (1914-1922) is the pope who has done the most to promote the Holy Family devotion. In his *Bonum Sane* (1920), he "affirms that the future of society depends on the family, and that the only hope for a renewed society is vigorous family life. Imitation of the Holy Family is the primary means to strengthen family life, because Jesus, Mary, and Joseph are 'marvelous exemplars of virtue' who 'should serve as inspiration and as models for all Christian families.' Benedict esteemed the Holy Family devotion as having primacy among all the Church's devotions. For him it is the 'pearl of devotions.' A year after *Bonum Sane*, on 26 October, 1921, Benedict made the Feast of the Holy Family obligatory for the Universal Church.

This progressively richer understanding of the Holy Family culminates in the consolidation of three crowning insights: the Holy Family's relationship to the Holy Trinity, the recognition of its role in our becoming a part of God's family, and its implications for the modern family as epitomized in Fatima, the apparition of the Holy Family (an apparition that took place during the papacy of Benedict XV).

The Gospel Code – *the Holy Family–Holy Trinity Nexus*

The most mysterious dimension of the Holy Family is its startling "connection" to the Holy Trinity. A link of a kind becomes evident even to those who read Scripture at the most superficial level. Jesus, after all, is the Son of God, the Second Person of the Trinity – although he is also a human being and the son of Joseph and Mary. Mary "was found with child through the holy Spirit" – one of the many ways in which Scripture links her to the Holy Spirit. Joseph was the earthly father of Jesus and, as such, served as the representative of the Heavenly Father. But those who read the Scriptures through the eyes of the Apocrypha had no hope of comprehending this subtle but supremely sublime "connection." Only liberation from those self-imposed straitjackets made it possible to explore the truths hidden in full sight.

And once we discover the scriptural Holy Family, we are led to an ineffable insight: the Holy Family mirrors the Holy Trinity on earth. This truth, we said, had been grasped by such great mystical Doctors of the Church as St. Teresa of Avila and St. John of the Cross and saints like Francis de Sales and Alphonsus Ligouri. But while the insight is not new it is little known. This is unfortunate because we are dealing with a truth that is urgent for our daily life and for eternity. It is an insight that enables us to gain a fuller understanding of the Trinity on the level of intellect and imagination. And, as these great saints have also pointed out, we become Christians in the full sense only if we have entered Nazareth.

We might even see the Holy Family as the divinely instituted pathway for "picturing" the Holy Trinity. The truth that God is Trinity, Three Persons subsisting in the unity of one divine Nature, is the greatest possible revelation and one that can only be known because it was revealed by God. And yet a constant challenge for the faithful is the problem of visualizing the Persons of the Trinity. Mental images of a man with a white beard, a man with a brown beard and a dove are not true visualizations of the Father, the Son or the Holy Spirit. These are anthropomorphic projections wrestling with a wholly transcendent reality. So how do you visualize the divine Persons?

The divine solution is given in the Holy Family of Nazareth. We cannot possibly visualize the Father, Son and Holy Spirit not only because they are purely spiritual but because they are infinite in being. Just as bewildering, they are self-existent, subsisting without beginning or end. But God has given an icon of his Triune Reality that helps engage intellect and imagination. The truest, the most potent and poignant possible likeness of the Holy Trinity in created reality is the Holy Family of Nazareth.

This "connection" is evident at several levels. We will start with the Gospels themselves.

The link between the Holy Family and the Holy Trinity might, in fact, be called Gospel truth. In *True Devotion to St. Joseph and the Church*, Dominic de Domenico points out that St. Joseph and the Father are highlighted and connected in the Gospel of Matthew, Mary and the Holy Spirit in Luke and Jesus as Son of Man and Son of God in Mark. Fittingly, the individual introductions to the Three Persons concludes with an ever-enduring meditation on the Holy Trinity in the Fourth Gospel. We quote from this work at some length below:

The Beginning

"To compare the Holy Family with the Holy Trinity, let us go back to the beginning of this relationship. The beginning is to be found in the mystery of the Annunciation. In this mystery two things take place; the Most Holy Trinity reveal themselves together for the first time, and the Holy Family is created.

The angel reveals the Holy Trinity in these words: "He will be great and he will be called the Son of the Most High…The Holy Spirit will come upon you, and the power of the most High will overshadow you; therefore the child to be born will be called holy, the Son of God." (Lk. 1:32, 35)

Although the name "Father" is not explicitly used, it is clearly implied by the word "Son." For there cannot be a son without a father or parent. The Holy Spirit is explicitly revealed to Mary. As for creation of the earthly trinity, clearly, since the marriage of Joseph and Mary already existed, the conception of Jesus necessarily brings the earthly trinity into existence as a family.

That the most Holy Trinity be made known and that the earthly trinity be created in the same event is not a coincidence. For it is through the earthly trinity that our minds can go up to the Most Holy Trinity. It is through the earthly trinity that we enter the life of the Most Holy trinity. It is by the earthly trinity that the divine life of the Most Holy Trinity enters us.

Where the Holy Family is found, there the Most Holy Trinity will be more perfectly received. For the earthly trinity is the most fertile soil in which the Most Holy Trinity may take root. These things can happen in degrees as one member of the Holy Family is present in the soul, more so as two are present, and most perfectly as all three persons are preset in the soul. Jesus can be there without Mary or Joseph. If Mary is here, then Jesus must be there, but not necessarily Joseph. If Joseph is there, then Jesus and Mary must necessarily be there also. For he cannot be thought of apart from them. Thus, the earthly trinity is conceived in the heart. From here the soul is launched more perfectly into the mystery of the Most Holy Trinity."

St. Matthew – the Gospel of the Heavenly Father and St. Joseph

"Is there some one thing that distinguishes the added material in each Gospel from the added material in the other Synoptic Gospels, and therefore characterizes each Gospel as distinct from the other Synoptic Gospels? The answer is affirmative. The Gospel of St. Matthew gives special emphasis to the Father and father-related ideas. For example, this Gospel begins with the genealogy of Christ, a list of fathers.

The only other genealogy found in the Gospels is in St. Luke, a list of sons, and it follows the infancy narrative, a less dominant position.

In the first sentence of the genealogy of St. Matthew, Jesus is called the son of David. The main point is to show that David is His father. From the very start the theme of father is a dominant one but with special emphasis on King David. His name is mentioned five times in the genealogy. Abraham is mentioned three times. No one else is mentioned more than twice. After first mentioning David, St. Matthew immediately refers to Jesus as the son of Abraham, who, in a special way, is considered the father of Israel, as also of many nations.

All those named in the genealogy of Matthew are fathers who beget sons, except Joseph and Jesus. This list of fathers ends with Jesus. In St. Luke, the genealogy is the reverse, beginning with Jesus and proceeding back to Adam and God. The emphasis is on each person as a son rather than as a father.

The genealogy of St. Matthew shows that Jesus is a king, and His kingship has its roots or origin in fatherhood. For kingship is an extension of the role of father. The king is the head of his people. The father is the head of his family. The king has authority and rules over his people. The father has authority and rules over his family. As the nation has its beginning in the family, so does kingship have its beginning in fatherhood.

This hidden subject, who begets Jesus, becomes more explicit in the next chapter, "Out of Egypt I called my son." (2:15) God Himself is the only father of Jesus. In God the Father we see the special light in which we behold the Gospel of St. Matthew. In Him is the source of fatherhood.

Moreover, in Him is the source of kingship. Later in the Gospel, during the Sermon on the Mount, Jesus will teach the Our Father. In this prayer we say, "Thy kingdom come." Thus, the Father is necessarily king. So, His Son is an heir to the kingship, and in the equality of the Holy trinity already shares in it. The kingdom of God will be the major theme of the entire Gospel, but it cannot be understood apart from the Father who is in Heaven.

If, then, Jesus is begotten by the Father, how is He the son of David? St. Matthew immediately provides the answer. The angel appears to

Joseph in a dream and addresses him: "Joseph, son of David…" (1:20) The title "son of David" is a very important one here, for by it, Joseph becomes the link between David and Jesus. The angel will go on to ask Joseph to take Mary his wife and to accept the role of a father toward Jesus. This fatherhood of St. Joseph provides Jesus with His legal ancestry. (This is not to exclude the possible link with David through His Mother.)

It can be said that Joseph is here being asked to be the visible representative of the Father. Not only that, but the infancy narrative in St. Matthew is from the point of view of St. Joseph who has this role of a father. For example, the angel appears to Joseph in dreams on four different occasions, rather than to Mary. This is in contrast with St. Juke's infancy narrative, which is from Mary's point of view. Thus again we see the distinct emphasis on fatherhood in St. Matthew.

Finally, it can be said that the Father gives the distinctive personality to this Gospel. Also, in a unique way, the Father is represented by St. Joseph who appears in the forefront in this Gospel only. In St. Luke he appears more

St. Mark – the Gospel of the Son of God and the Son of Man

"As St. Matthew is characterized by the father and Joseph, so also St. Mark is characterized by the Son Who is Jesus. St. Mark commences his Gospel with these words, "The beginning of the Good News about Jesus Christ, the Son of God." (1:1) St. Luke makes no reference at all to Jesus Christ at the beginning of his Gospel. Only St. Mark calls Him the Son of God in the beginning of his Gospel. Already we have the clue that this is the Gospel of the Son.

There is no infancy narrative in St. Mark. Thus the only person in the Holy Family to receive serious attention is Jesus. Most of the doctrine and sayings of Jesus are absent from St. Mark. This further emphasizes the Person of Jesus Christ. Therefore Jesus Himself is the only message and focus of St. Mark.

Still, in St. Mark, Jesus only refers to Himself as the Son of Man. He especially does this regarding His Passion, which is only possible because He is also a man. (Here one aspect of the title "Son of Man" is given, without prejudice to the other possible aspects of the title.) In this way, Jesus is identified not only as the second Person of the Most Holy Trinity, the Son of God, but also as a member of the human family. Within the context of the three Synoptic Gospels, He is seen as a member of the Holy Family. St. Mark says: "This is the carpenter, surely, the son of Mary,…" (6:3) Thus, the synoptic Matthew, Mark, and Luke represent not only the Father, Son, and, as we shall see, the Holy Spirit, but also Joseph, Jesus as man, and , as we shall see, Mary."

St. Luke – the Gospel of the Holy Spirit and Mary

"St. Luke is the Gospel of the Holy Spirit. Unlike the other two Gospels there is no reference to Jesus Christ at the beginning of the Gospel. Instead St. Luke speaks of his decision to write an ordered account. Since the writing of Holy Scripture is a work attributable to the inspiration of the Holy Spirit, and since it is in such an outward work that the Holy Spirit is revealed to us, one might see in this beginning, at least a reference to something associated with the action of the Holy Spirit Himself.

St. Luke is also the Gospel that sees things from Mary's point of view. The Blessed Virgin would have been the original source for the infancy narrative. St. Luke describes her: "His Mother stored up all these things in her heart." (2:52)

There is more about Our Lady in this Gospel than in any other. Yet, Our Lady is not merely more prominent in this Gospel. There is also here a very close association of Mary with the Holy Spirit. The angel names her "full of grace." Grace is the means through which the Holy Spirit acts in each person. We can deduce then that she acts under his influence in all things. Where we find Mary, we find the Holy Spirit. In seeing her we see the Holy Spirit insofar as that is possible. In her we see the motherly expressions of the Holy Spirit, so to speak. Hence she is a visible representation of the Holy Spirit."

The Synoptics – Holy Trinity and Holy Family

"It may be concluded then that the Synoptic Gospels represent primarily the Most Holy Trinity, and subordinately, the Holy Family or earthly trinity. Like these two trinities, although each in a different way, the Synoptics are one Gospel because of their common message or material and yet three distinct Gospels with their own special emphases.

The Gospel of St. Matthew represents the Father and St. Joseph. St. Mark represents the Son of God Who is Jesus. St. Luke represents the Holy Spirit and the Blessed Mother. In this there is the implication that the Holy Family is the visible representation of the Most Holy Trinity.

This is not a message that is found on some particular page, in some particular chapter. Still, it is a message communicated by all three Synoptic Gospels standing together as a whole. It is a message that gives the framework within which these Gospels are written."

St. John – Gospel of the Holy Trinity

"The Gospel of St. John brings together all three divine Persons, and allows us to look indirectly but explicitly into the inner life of the Most Holy Trinity.

St. John does not do the same with the Holy Family. There is one reference to St. Joseph. (1:45) It seems that the Synoptic Gospels, rooted in the earthly trinity, provided the launching platform from which we could fly with the wings of an eagle into the highest doctrine of the Most Holy Trinity. Having prepared the way, the Synoptics achieved their purpose by disposing and enabling us to contemplate and live the inner life of the Most Holy Trinity."

Comparing Holy Trinity and Holy Family

"In comparing these two trinities we must realize that they are not totally and completely other or distinct. For in these two trinities there is a total of five persons. One of these five persons is common to both trinities, namely, Jesus Christ. Thus the Holy Family includes a divine Person. Yet, insofar as the Holy Family is created and mediates with God for us by reason of all that is human, the Holy Trinity infinitely surpasses the Holy Family.

Further, our understanding of the Holy Trinity does not originate in the Holy Family. Rather, the Holy family represents the Holy Trinity insofar as the earthly trinity conforms to its likeness. One could very easily fall into error by attempting to reverse this by attempting to conform the Holy Trinity to the Holy Family. This comparison then presupposes that one has a well-developed theology of the Holy Trinity beforehand. This is not to deny possible new insights that lay hidden in the deposit of faith.

Still, it is to be understood that Joseph does not generate Jesus in any way, such as a natural father generates a child or as the heavenly Father generates His divine Son. For St. Joseph was intended to represent the Father, not to take His place. Some then, have called St. Joseph the vicar or shadow of the Father.

Nor should we think of St. Joseph as representing the Father to the same degree as Jesus and Mary represent the other divine Persons. For as we shall see, there is no equality among the members of the Holy family, either as representatives of the divine Persons or otherwise, except by reason of human nature. In regard to this human nature, like all people, St. Joseph is an image of the Triune God.

On the other hand, Jesus is not simply a representation of the Son of God; He is the Son of God, "God from God Light from Light, true God from true God." (Nicene Creed) Jesus is able to represent a Divine Person in a sense, by reason of His human nature which in and of itself is not God but is like God. That is not all. Jesus even more perfectly represents the Father than does St. Joseph. For He is the perfect image of the Father. All others are but imperfect images of God. The Gospel of St. John confirms that Jesus is a representation of the Father: "To have seen me is to have seen the Father." (14:9)

Is there a need for St. Joseph to represent the Father if Jesus fulfills this more perfectly? Within the Holy Trinity and within the Holy Family, Jesus is the Son. A son, as such, is not a Father, Sonship, as such, cannot represent fatherhood. In this sense, St. Joseph as a father himself is more suitable to represent the Father, especially within the Holy family, although imperfectly.

Our Blessed mother represents the Holy Spirit in a way different from the way either Jesus represents Himself or Joseph represents another Person. She is not a divine Person, as is Jesus. Yet, on the other hand, she represents the Holy Spirit in a way far superior to that of St. Joseph's representation of the Father.

Through the Immaculate Conception no stain of sin was allowed to touch her, and ever did her heart remain immaculate. As a result, there was never anything in her but what was of the Holy Spirit, even in her natural being of which God is the first cause. Thus one could say of her, "To see Mary is to see the Holy Spirit," insofar as that is possible. God even named her *kecharitomene*, full of grace. Since grace is attributed to the Holy Spirit, it can be said that even in her name, which signifies her person and mission, she is intimately associated with the Holy Spirit.

Was there, then, something which united the Holy Family in an exclusive way? Was there something that united them to one another while setting them apart from others as the Holy Trinity is apart? The answer is to be found in matrimony, and, in their case, holy matrimony. For they were joined together by God Himself as the beginning and end of their marriage. God brought them together and the God-man was the fruit of their marriage. Thus husband and wife were united in the exclusive bond of marriage with Jesus as the offspring. In addition, these bonds required a special kind of knowing and loving among the members of the family. Thus these family relationships required a love which had priority over the love given to those outside the nuclear family. It is in the human family that human persons first begin to become a visible sign of the Holy Trinity, not only in forming a trinity of persons with each child, but in their exclusive oneness.

Finally, there is the order of father, mother, and child. This might be the order a person might consider first, only to be discouraged by the fact that the mother is placed in the same position as the Son in the Holy Trinity. Still, Mary represents the motherly aspects of Christ found appropriately in the book of Luke. "How often I would have gathered your children together as a hen gathers her brood under her wings, and you would not!" (13:34, cf. Mt. 23:37) Another problem is that the mother does not proceed from the father, nor is she generated by the father as is the second Person in the Holy Trinity. Moreover, the child is generated by the father and mother. The Holy Spirit is not generated by the Father and Son. The procession of the Holy Spirit from the Father and the Son is called spiration. As the desire of the will is different from the conception of an idea in the intellect, so is spiration different from generation. For the desire or love from the will is analogous to the spiration of the Holy Spirit. The conception of an idea is analogous to the spiritual generation of the Word.

Nonetheless, there are some similarities between the temporal order of the family and the Holy Trinity. The child proceeds from the union of two persons, as does the Holy Spirit. Thus the child is an imperfect likeness of the Holy Spirit by reason of the fact that both proceed from two persons. Also there is a similarity in the love between the first two persons. The love between two human persons is made visible in a third person, the child, as the Holy Spirit is the personified Love between two persons. Yet there is no likeness in the way they proceed, one by generation and the other by spiration. (Cf. n. 578) Also revelation seems to represent love more by the mother than by the child. Clearly the temporal order of the family is less able to represent the Holy Trinity than the above explanations. For the first two explanations were based on the spiritual order, while the latter explanation was more dependent on the physical order which less perfectly reflects God. However, any comparison to the Holy Trinity is necessarily imperfect. Still, the comparison is quite useful for our understanding and devotion....

Every family ordinarily desires to continue itself in future generations through offspring. The Holy Family was really no different in this regard, except that it was done in a higher way. In the genealogy of St. Matthew, Jesus is at the end of many generations. The hereditary line ends. Jesus does not procreate according to the flesh. Yet, it is the beginning of a new line of spiritual rebirth and of a kingdom that will have no end. Jesus, Mary, and Joseph, all virgins, labored in love for the extension and continuation of their Holy Family. In this sense, the Holy Family was more than simply a family. This family was ordained to be the model and the beginning of the Church. Since the Holy Family is the Church in its origin, it follows that the Church partakes in the Trinitarian nature of the Holy Family."[17]

Mapping the Earthly and Heavenly Families

The scriptural architecture is supplemented by the theological portrait of Jesus, Mary and Joseph in Christian history. Each member of the Holy Family is encountered and situated in relation to an infinite Person of the Holy Trinity. (Please note that "Person" as applied to the Trinity is used analogously. A Trinitarian Person is not like a finite super-person: rather the noun is used to identify an infinite-eternal relationship within God). The parallel between the earthly and heavenly families means that each member of the Holy Family is, in some sense, "connected" to a specific divine Person. Thus, Jesus is the divine Logos/Son, Mary images the Holy Spirit and Joseph is the representative of the Father.

Jesus – the divine Logos/Son

Jesus is not simply an image of the Second Person: he *is* the Second Person. But there is another level that should not be overlooked. The human Jesus embodies precisely in his human nature the "truth", so to speak, of his divine nature as Son of God. It has been said that only the Son could have become incarnate because the divine Person in his historical action reflects his reality in the eternal: the Son is sent from the Father because he eternally proceeds from the Father.

St. Joseph – Representative of the Father

To begin with, it is surely significant that the Heavenly Father entrusted the safety and well-being of his only-begotten Son to this just and ever-obedient man whom the boy Jesus called "Abba" which literally means "Daddy." Joseph was the "representative" of the Father (we say representative because no human person is ultimately comparable to the uncreated Creator).

Said Pope John Paul II:

> "In Joseph, called to be the earthly father of the incarnate Word, *the divine fatherhood is reflected in a most extraordinary way.* Joseph is the father of Jesus because he is really Mary's husband. She conceived virginally through God's action, but the child is also the son of Joseph, her lawful husband. This is why in the Gospel both are called the "parents" of Jesus (Lk 2:27, 41).
>
> "Through the exercise of his fatherhood, Joseph cooperates, in the fullness of time, in the great mystery of salvation (cf. *Redemptoris*

Custos, n. 8). "His fatherhood is expressed concretely in his having made his life a service ... to the mystery of the Incarnation and to the redemptive mission connected with it; ... in having turned his human vocation to domestic love into a superhuman oblation of self, an oblation of his heart and all his abilities into love placed at the service of the Messiah growing up in his house" (ibid.). To this end, God shared his own fatherly love with Joseph, that love "from [which] every family in heaven and on earth is named" (Eph 3:15).

"Like every child, Jesus learned about life and how to act from his parents. How could we not think, with deep wonder, that he must have developed the human aspect of his perfect obedience to the Father's will particularly by following the example of his father Joseph, "a just man" (cf. Mt 1:19)." Angelus, March 21, 1999

"Joseph, son of David, do not fear to take Mary and that which is conceived in her (cf. MT 1:20). So God the Father says to the man with whom, in a way, he shared his fatherhood. God, dear brothers, in a sense shares his fatherhood with each of you. Not in the mysterious and supernatural way in which he did with Joseph of Nazareth." Mass on the Feast of St. Joseph, March 19, 1981

In a memorable meditation, Jean-Jacques Olier, the protégé of St. Vincent de Paul and St. Francis de Sales mentioned earlier with reference to Montreal, points out that:

> "The admirable St. Joseph was given to the earth to express the adorable perfection of God the Father in a tangible way. In his person alone, he bore the beauties of God the Father, his purity and love, his wisdom and prudence, his mercy and compassion. One saint alone is destined to represent God the Father while an infinite number of creatures, a multitude of saints are needed to represent Jesus Christ. For the work of the whole Church is solely to give an outward manifestation of the virtues and the perfection of its adorable head and St. Joseph alone represents the eternal Father … The Father having chosen this saint to make of him his image on earth, gives him along with himself a likeness of his invisible and hidden nature and, in my view, this saint is beyond the state of being understood by the minds of humans." "The Son of God, having made himself visible by taking on human flesh, conversed and visibly dealt with God his Father,

in the person of St. Joseph, by whom the Father made himself visible to him."

Pope John XXIII calls St. Joseph the "shadow of the Father":

> Christmas is the great family feast. In coming upon earth to save human society and restore it to its high destiny, Jesus manifested himself with Mary his mother, with Joseph his putative father who is there as the shadow of the eternal Father. Thus was the great restoration of the entire world begun." 1959 Christmas message,

The theological foundations of St. Joseph's likeness to the Father are outlined by Joaquín Ferrer Arellano:

> In the light of the Scotistic thesis on the Primacy of Christ, to take one example, one discovers (...) how the virginal marriage of Mary and Joseph was predestined "ante mundi constitutionem" (before the constitution of the world), as an essential part of the one decree of the Incarnation of the Word in the womb of the Immaculate "ante praevisa merita" (before any consideration of antecedent merit). Such is the saving plan, "the mystery hidden before the ages in God," (cf. Eph 3:9) to be accomplished at the high point in the history of salvation. That high point is the fullness of time (cf. Gal

4:4) when God sent his Son into the most pure bosom of Holy Mary Ever Virgin, espoused to a man of the house of David (cf. Lk 1:26) in fulfillment of the prophecy of Nathan. God acted thus, that through the obedience of the Spouses of Nazareth the Son might be freely welcomed into history on behalf of all mankind in order to save it. This welcome took place in the virginal womb of Mary, the Daughter of Zion, and in the house of Joseph, in the family home established by the marriage of the two Spouses (Mary and Joseph), "sanctuary of love and cradle of life." This is the theological foundation of the holy Patriarch's greatness as virginal, messianic father of the Only-begotten of the Father: shadow and transparent icon of Him who wished to make Joseph unique partaker of his fatherhood in order to prepare the human nature of Christ for the holocaust of Calvary. In this way, He made Joseph Father and Lord of the Church gushing forth from Christ's opened side and born of the sword of sorrow of the Woman.[17]

Mary – Spouse and Image of the Spirit

Finally, there is the Blessed Virgin Mary, the human person most closely identified with the Holy Spirit throughout Christian history. We have already seen the scriptural, conciliar and liturgical foundations of this identification of the Blessed Virgin with the Third Person of the Trinity.

Other great Christian thinkers, past and present, further explored Mary's link to the Holy Spirit. St. Maximilian Kolbe drew a correlation between Mary's identity as the Immaculate Conception and the identity of the Holy Spirit as the Uncreated Immaculate Conception. Who is the Holy Spirit? He is the fruit of the love of the Father and the Son. The fruit of created love is a created conception. But the fruit of the love that is the prototype of created love (likewise) is none other than a Conception. The Spirit is therefore the uncreated eternal Conception which is "the prototype of all the conceptions that multiply life throughout the whole universe." The Holy Spirit is "this infinitely holy, Immaculate Conception." Thus Mary as immaculate conception complements the Holy Spirit who is the uncreated Conception.

Kolbe then explored the intellectual consequences of this parallel: "The Second Person of the Most Holy Trinity came upon the earth and gave us the proof of his love. The Third Person of the Trinity is not incarnated. Nevertheless, the expression 'Spouse of the Holy Spirit' is very much more profound than human concepts can express." Certainly *Mary is not literally an "incarnation" of the Spirit* since they remain distinct persons, one human, the other divine. As Kolbe clarifies, "He [the Holy Spirit] is in the Immaculata as the Second Person of the most Holy Trinity, the Word, is in Jesus Christ – with this difference: in Jesus we have two natures, the divine and the human; but the nature and person of the Immaculata are different from the nature and person of the Holy Spirit." And yet, "It is an unexplainable but perfect union by reason of which the Holy Spirit does not act except through the Immaculata, his Spouse. She therefore is the Mediatrix of all the graces of the Most Holy Spirit." There is no question, of course, of obscuring the work of the Spirit. Kolbe goes so far as to say, "Our Lady exists so that the name of the Holy Spirit may be better known."

Eastern Orthodox thinkers had a similarly profound understanding. Said Sergius Bulgakov: "The Annunciation was a complete and therefore hypostatic descent of the Holy Spirit with his entry to the Virgin Mary ... by his coming into the Virgin Mary he identifies himself in a way with her through her God-motherhood ... he does not at all leave her after the birth of Christ, but remains forever with her in the full force of the Annunciation." Again, this is not a literal incarnation but as the same author says, "He abides, however, in the ever-

Virgin Mary as in a holy temple, while her human personality seems to become transparent to him and to provide him with a human countenance." A few hours before his death, the Orthodox scholar Paul Evdokimov wrote, "The Holy Spirit has no place of incarnation, but he possesses in Mary the unique and altogether distinctive temple of his presence."

All these insights have a direct bearing on Mary's role in the divinizing mission of the Spirit as pointed out by the Orthodox Father Theophanes of Nicaea (d.1381): "Through her we gave our nature to God the Word; therefore the divinity that is bestowed on us truly through her is given. Just as she gave our nature directly to God the Word, so God the Word to her directly repaid the deification of all; just as the Son of God through the mediation of his own Mother receives from us our own nature, so through her mediation we receive his deification." Mary was able to become the Mother of the Son only because of the Spirit: "Without the divine Spirit and his partnership it is impossible for a created nature in any way to approach the Son." "The Mother of the Son" is in fact "the image of the Paraclete." "Of such a kind and so great are the union and coalition of the Paraclete with the most holy Virgin that no language can explain them, no mind grasp them." Her mission manifests his: "She receives wholly the hidden grace of the Spirit and amply distributes it and shares it with others, thus manifesting it."

Mary was the first person to be divinized. This happened as a direct result of (a) the decree of the Father of whom she was "the highly favored daughter" (b) the incarnation of the Son who was also her Son and (c) the total indwelling of the Holy Spirit who became thereby her Spouse. Uniquely, as the Fathers of the Church have said, she is the image and icon of the Spirit. From this, we realize that the role of Mary can be grasped only when we understand the Holy Spirit. Conversely, the more we understand Mary, the better we understand the workings of the Holy Spirit. Thus, all the appearances of Mary in history and all Marian doctrine and devotion are directly related to the divinizing mission of the Spirit.

Entering the Family of God

The dimension of divinization draws us into the urgent relevance of the Holy Family in our lives. We find this at three levels:

- The mission of the Holy Family in human history and the world
- The part played by the Holy Family in our own salvation and sanctification
- The role of the Holy Family in drawing us into the life of the Holy Trinity

We will consider each in turn.

World History

The mission of the Holy Family did not stop with the Gospel events. The Holy Family is certainly a model for all families to emulate but, above and beyond the "icon" dimension, Jesus, Mary and Joseph are active here-and-now, across history, across the world. To the extent we become aware of their presence and action, to that extent we can participate in the designs of Providence and avail ourselves of its embedded blessings. Once we learn the laws of nature, we can apply those laws in the creation of valuable technologies while also learning newer truths: this is just as true in the spiritual world as it is in the physical. And just as the laws of motion are true and binding whether or not we discover them, so also the action of the Holy Family continues whether or not we recognize it.

Occasionally, Heaven does unveil the presence of the Family in the midst of the here and now. Thus, at Fatima the apparition of Mary is accompanied by a vision of Joseph and Jesus blessing the world. At Knock and Zeitoun too we see the entire Holy Family.

The very real link between the Holy Family and salvation history is, of course, laid out already in the Gospels where we are given a glimpse of the pivotal role played by Joseph and Mary in the Incarnation of the Redeemer. The gradual re-discovery of Joseph and subsequently the Holy Family in Christian history highlighted the continued reality of this link. The Church has joyously risen to the occasion. Particularly memorable are the words of Pope John XXIII already cited, one of the greatest papal champions of St. Joseph: "St. Joseph is the protector par excellence of the family, along with the other two of whom he was the incomparable guardian. The simple mention of Jesus, Mary and Joseph reminds us that there [in the Holy Family] **we find all human history** and there we find also the salvation, the grandeur, the beauty, the splendor of the Catholic Church."

We are Family

Salvation history is targeted toward our salvation here and now. The goal of human life on earth is to live eternally with the Author of life. But to live with God we must have the Life of God. This means being "divinized," i.e., receiving the divine Life as the New Testament testifies ("I live, no longer I, but Christ lives in me"). Divinizing is of the utmost importance since we must be divinized here and now to live hereafter with God. Thus, we are all called to live with the divine Life and this entails entering the family of God.

The importance of family is clear in the Scriptures. "Every house is founded by someone, but the founder of all is God. Moses was "faithful in all his house" as a "servant" to testify to what would be spoken, but Christ was faithful as a son placed over his house. We are his house, if [only] we hold fast to our confidence and pride in our hope." (Hebrews 3: 4-6) The human vocation is a call to become members of the family of God. For the Son of God became the Son of man so that humankind might enter "the household of God." (Ephesians 2:19).

To become part of the household of God is to become part of the family of God incarnate. Why? It is only by taking on our humanity that the eternal

Logos can gift us a partaking of his divine nature: divinization: that is to say, we "come to share in the divine nature." (2 Peter 1: 4).

At this point, we see why the Holy Family is, in fact, a living bridge between humanity and the Holy Trinity: all those who are the children of Joseph and Mary via the human nature of Jesus become the sons and daughters of the Father via the divine nature of Jesus of which they partake (2 Peter 1:4) through the Holy Spirit. The human family of Jesus is, above all, the family that does the will of the heavenly Father: the father being the ever-obedient "just man," the mother "the handmaid of the Lord" and the Son the One who "learned obedience from what he suffered" (Hebrews 5:8). All who say Yes to the Father in Heaven become part of this family consecrated to God: "Whoever does the will of my heavenly Father is my brother, and sister, and mother." (Matthew 12: 50).

The formula is actually simple. In point of fact, whether we know it or not, every relationship with Jesus is a relationship with the Holy Family. Jesus receives his human nature from Mary. Mary, by virtue of her marriage to him, is of "one flesh" with Joseph. Thus Jesus is the son not just of Mary but (at the level of divine law) of Joseph. Mary was proclaimed the Mother of God because she is physically the mother of an infinite Person in his human nature. All those who accept Jesus have a human relationship with Jesus via his human nature. But Jesus is an infinite (i.e., divine) Person with both a human and a divine nature and our relationship is thus also with his divine nature. And since Mary is the mother of this infinite divine Person in his humanity and likewise Joseph is his father, and since our relationship with Jesus to be real has to be one of being his *human* brother or sister, we therefore become children of Joseph and Mary. This is why the Bible pointedly says that the "offspring" of the Woman Clothed with the Sun who is mother of the Messiah (i.e., Mary) are "those who keep God's commandments and bear witness to Jesus." (*Revelation* 12:17). There is nothing exceptional in this emphasis on becoming part of a "chosen" family. Salvation history in Scripture is a matter of families: Adam and his family, then Noah with his family and finally Abraham the father of the people of Israel who become the People of God. The only difference is that the family of Jesus starts in time and ends in eternity. And it is a family that all are invited to join.

So how do you become part of the Holy Family? By virtue of our baptism, we are de facto members of this family because through the indwelling of the Holy Spirit we become brothers and sisters of Jesus and children of the Father. Jesus give us his mother as our spiritual mother and his virginal father as our spiritual father. Through their guidance and intercession, we are continually molded into the likeness of their Son and Savior. Just as the Holy Spirit acted in our lives before we became aware of the Holy Spirit, so also the Holy Family is present with all who "bear witness to Jesus" whether they are aware of it or not.

The relation of the Holy Family to the Church becomes evident here. The New Testament tells us that the Church is the household of God: "the household of God, which is the church of the living God." (1 Timothy 3:16.) The Church, at its very beginning, is the Holy Family. Over time, the brothers and sisters of Jesus are adopted into this Family. But the human father and mother of the Son are the earthly spiritual father and mother of all those who are brothers and sisters of the Son. For this reason we say that St. Joseph is the Protector and Patron of the Church and the Blessed Virgin the Mother of the Church. Accordingly, Pius IX had proclaimed St. Joseph's patronage of the Church and Paul VI defined the Virgin Mary as the Mother of the Church.

The Church is also called the Body of Christ. The Body of Christ, in fact, manifests Itself at three levels and all are linked to his Family. There is the natural body of Jesus of Nazareth, his mystical body which is the Church and his sacramental body, the Eucharist. The Anglican theologian Eric Mascall points out that all three are tied to the Mother of Jesus (and thus implicitly to his earthly father).

> Mary is the mother of Jesus and of those who are incorporated into him, the mother of the Church which is his Mystical Body and which, because a man and his bride are one flesh, is also Christ's bride. ... When the Spirit descended in tongues of fire, it was to make the waiting group into the mystical Body of Christ in a way analogous to that in which the descent of the Spirit upon Mary at her Annunciation had formed the natural body of Christ in her womb. Nevertheless, although the Mystical Body came into being by this new descent of the Spirit, *there was not a new incarnation*, Christ was not becoming man a second time, he was not assuming a new nature; the human nature which he had taken from his mother, in which he had died for our sins and risen again for our justification, was being made present under a new mode. *There are not, strictly speaking, two bodies of Christ, a natural and a mystical, but one body of Christ which is manifested in two forms.*

Nor does the story end here, for that part of the Mystical Body which is on earth needs to be continually nourished and sustained, as Christ's natural body did before its glorification. It is through the Eucharistic Body of the Blessed Sacrament that this takes place. Here again, there is not a new incarnation, but *in the Eucharist the human nature which Christ took from his mother is made present in yet another form*, a form through which that part of the Mystical Body which is still *in via* on earth is repeatedly sustained and renewed.

In all these modes of manifestation, the human nature of Christ is the human nature which he took from Mary.

The descent of the Holy Spirit on Mary at the Annunciation first formed it, the descent of the Holy Spirit upon the Apostles at Pentecost released it, so to speak, in the world as the Mystical Body of the Church, and *the descent of the Holy Spirit upon the Eucharistic elements brings it to us as the Sacramental Body*.

But in all these manifestations and expressions, it is one and the same Body, the Body which was formed in Mary's womb, and so when we return from the Altar, having received the sacramental Body of Christ and having thereby been received more firmly into his Mystical Body, we can say with a new emphasis the words that, in the Genesis story, Adam said after he had tasted the food given him by the first Eve: 'The woman gave me, and I did eat' (Gen 3:12).

For it is the very body, the human nature, which Christ took from his mother, on which we are fed in the Holy Eucharist.[18]

Trinitarian Takeaway

Finally, to become part of the Holy Family is to enter the Family of God, the Holy Trinity. The Holy Family is a portal into the Holy Trinity. The Incarnation of God in Jesus Christ reveals to us that God is Family – Father, Son and the Love between the Two that is the Holy Spirit. ("God in his deepest mystery is not a solitude but a family, since he has in himself fatherhood, sonship and the essence of the family which is love."—John Paul II[19]). The divine Family sends us the Holy Family for it is through this Family that the Word becomes Incarnate thereby enabling us to become adopted sons and daughters of the Father through the indwelling of the Holy Spirit.

We have already seen that the Holy Family is an earthly image of the Holy Trinity – St. Joseph, the representative of the Father; Jesus the divine Son incarnate; the Blessed Virgin Mary, the Spouse of the Holy Spirit. Pope Benedict XVI rightly said:

"The Holy Family of Nazareth [is] the harmonious reflection on earth of the life of the Most Holy Trinity." (October 2011)

At a basic level every family reflects the divine Family. As St. John Paul II put it: "Humanity images God in the family."[20] Again, "[God] willed man and woman to be the prime community of persons, source of every other community, and, at the same time, to be a 'sign' of that interpersonal communion of love which constitutes the mystical, intimate life of God, One in Three."[21]

The discovery of the Holy Family has been accompanied in parallel by a radically new understanding of the family itself. The same 20th century that saw the decimation of the family also, paradoxically, gave us a deeper insight into the nature of the family. There was, on the one hand, the development of the traditional idea of the family as the "domestic church."

But coupled with this there was the new realization of the Trinitarian dimension of both marriage and family: God the Holy Trinity not only being the original model of the family but the life of the Trinity "interpenetrating" the life of the family. Beyond marriage as a "legal" union is the understanding of it as a communion of persons. Beyond the untenable dualisms introduced between sex and spirituality (in ancient times) and conjugal union and procreation (in modern times) there has emerged a holistic awareness of divine participation in both marital union and human birth. Moreover, in discovering the Holy Trinity and the Holy Family, we come to see the full glory of the family. The family which is a mystery shrouded in darkness simply in natural terms (the origin of reproduction as such, unlike its structures, is biologically inexplicable) becomes a dazzling mystery of light at the supernatural level. The headline is the family both imaging the Trinity and being drawn into the Trinitarian dynamic. We see with new eyes the reality that always lay in plain sight before us.

While "new" in terms of explicit articulation, the seeds of the connection between the Trinity and the family were sown in Genesis: "God created mankind in his image; in the image of God he created them; male and female he created them. God blessed them and God said to them: Be fertile and multiply." (Genesis 1:27-8)

It has been pointed out that in this Genesis creation account, the likeness between God and creature lies in God who creates and man his creation, male and female, who procreates. God is imaged by a community. Moreover, as Marc Ouellet observes, "the deliberate plural 'Let us make,' which introduces the doctrine of image (man made in the image of God) in Genesis, when complemented with the New Testament revelation, gives us a solid scriptural basis upon which to found the family image of the Trinity."[22]

The rest of the Hebrew Bible is rich in its revelation of the family. As we have seen, families are front-and-center in God's interactions with humanity: the family of Adam, the family of Noah and, finally, the family of Abraham which becomes a nation and indeed the family of God (Israel my son). These families are bound to God by covenants (partnership agreements): the covenants with Adam, Noah, Abraham and Moses. Within the family of God there are families endowed with specialized covenants: the priestly family of Levi and the royal family of David.

In the New Covenant inaugurated by the Son of God made man, the family of God transcends the people of Israel and is "opened up" to all who accept the Redeemer of humanity as Lord and Savior. The New Covenant restores marriage to its original structure: what God has joined together let no man put asunder. What is more, the relationship between God and his people is now seen in terms of family. Jesus always call God Father and by becoming the adopted siblings of Jesus, we too become children of the Father. We are temples of the Holy Spirit.

Likewise, the Father and the Son dwell in us. And just as God is present in the marital union, so also the relationship of the Church to Christ is of bride and bridegroom.

Israel, the family of God, prefigures the Church as the family of God (Hebrews, Timothy) which in turn points to Heaven, the family of God in all its glory ("So then you are no longer strangers and sojourners, but you are fellow citizens with the holy ones and members of the household of God." (Ephesians 2:19)).

And it is this final celestial and eternal reality of the family that is embodied in the Holy Family of Nazareth.

The ultimacy of the family – it is eternal, it is where we go, it is who we are – manifests itself in the immediate, the here and now. It is not just a legal contract but a locus of God's action in the world, a participation in heavenly mysteries in the here and now. The timeless is mirrored in time. But what we make of ourselves in time ends up being what we are in the timeless. We cannot know the full truth about the family without considering it in the light of divinity and eternity.

Every family is called to live in three larger overlapping families: the Holy Family, the Church and the Holy Trinity. The launching pad is the Holy Family. Hence the need to re-discover the reality of its role and action and to make the Holy Family a part of our lives.

In his prophetic *Breve Neminem Fugit*, June 14, 1892, the Pope of the Holy Family, Pope Leo XIII, said

"The God of mercies, in carrying out the work of such a longed-for human redemption, chose to fulfill it in a way that its beginning would offer to the world a unique Family, divinely constituted, in which all peoples might contemplate the most accomplished model of family community and of full virtue and holiness. Such indeed was that Family of Nazareth wherein the Sun of Justice, Christ Jesus, our saving God, before revealing himself to the world in all his splendor, chose to remain hidden with the Virgin Mother and her most holy spouse Joseph, who carried out the role of his father.

The peace that accrues to family life from reciprocal love, an exemplary lifestyle and piety, flourished with the utmost splendor in that Holy Family, which was destined to be teaching and model of these family virtues for all families. Therefore, by divine disposition of Providence, it appeared to be structured in a way that every Christian, whatever one's state and situation in life, might, through contemplation, readily find in it inspiration and incentive for the practice of all the virtues."

The Holy Family is a great gift to us from the Savior, one which we would be wise to unwrap and embrace. The first step in doing so is the daily consecration to the Holy Family composed by Leo:

ACT OF CONSECRATION TO THE HOLY FAMILY

Prescribed by Pope Leo XIII

O Jesus, our most loving Redeemer, who having come to enlighten the world with Thy teaching and example, didst will to pass the greater part of Thy life in humility and subjection to Mary and Joseph in the poor home of Nazareth, thus sanctifying the Family that was to be an example for all Christian families, graciously receive our family as it dedicates and consecrates itself to Thee this day. Do Thou protect us, guard us and establish amongst us Thy holy fear, true peace and concord in Christian love: in order that by living according to the divine pattern of Thy family we may be able, all of us without exception, to attain to eternal happiness.

Mary, dear Mother of Jesus and Mother of us, by the kindly intercession make this our humble offering acceptable in the sight of Jesus, and obtain for us His graces and blessings.

O Saint Joseph, most holy Guardian of Jesus and Mary, help us by thy prayers in all our spiritual and temporal needs; that so we may be enabled to praise our divine Savior Jesus, together with Mary and thee, for all eternity.

All in the Family

The celestially-directed focus on the Holy Family we have reviewed enables us to re-discover the importance of marriage between man and woman and its fecund fulfillment in the family. Marriage and family were not only divinely instituted but reflect the inner Being of God – this is what has been revealed. Reproduction is a mystery that has no scientific explanation (John Maddox, editor of the journal Nature, said: "The overriding question is when (and then how) sexual reproduction itself evolved. Despite decades of speculation, we do not know."). Because it is so important for the continuation of the race, the reproductive act is a pleasurable one. But reproduction in the divine plan is situated exclusively within marriage and family. Both institutions are essential for the well-being of the human person and society as a whole. As such they should be supported and celebrated by all social and cultural institutions. The importance of the family can be illustrated by pointing to statistics or history but that is not where we should be looking. Rather, we should consider the time-tested conviction that the family is not a human construct. It derives from the fundamental fabric of reality.

Apart from imaging the very being of God, the family has been directly instituted by God. This is what the biblical record tells us. This is also what the different religions have said in their own way. At the inception of the human race, we are told that "God created man in his image; in the divine image he created him; male and female he created them." (Genesis 1:27) and that "a man leaves his father and mother and clings to his wife, and the two of them become one body." (Genesis 2:24) Ancient societies from the Arandas and Arabana of Australia to the great tribal nations of Africa to the Vedic Hindus to the ancient Chinese embedded marriage within intricate customs and rituals and observed elaborate rules relating to the family. Three of the Ten Commandments deal with specific obligations and prohibitions pertaining to husband, wife and family. Jesus took the primordial revelation about the family to a new plane when he said, "From the beginning of creation, 'God made them male and female. For this reason a man shall leave his father and mother (and be joined to his wife), and the two shall become one flesh.' ... *What God has joined together, no human being must separate.*" (Mark 10:6-9). So marriage under the Christian dispensation is a supernatural union.

In modern times, however, the institutions of marriage and family are under attack from all directions: academia, the media, the entertainment industry, the state, economic systems that treat it as a unit of production rather than as the foundational assets they should serve, industrial and technological revolutions, politicians, utopians. Under such powerful and sustained assaults, both institutions have fallen apart in societies across the world. And the results, have been catastrophic both for individuals and society.

Who are you? At the most basic level you are either a son or a daughter. You could also be husband, wife, father, mother, brother, sister, uncle, aunt, cousin, grandparent. Thus you belong to the immediate family into which you were born and its extensions. You belong also to the human family since all humans come from the same species with the same common ancestor. But you are called to be part of three other types of family although membership in each is strictly optional. These are the divine family (the Holy Trinity), the Holy Family and the covenant family (the Church). You are invited to join each of them but acceptance is entirely up to you. Membership in the five families has its own obligations and blessings. When you neglect your obligations you hurt yourself and often others as well. When a father abandons his family he causes suffering to each and every one in the family. When the first parents turned away from God, they unleashed untold suffering on the entire human family. Correspondingly, when you honor your obligations, you bring blessings on yourself and on others. When Abraham obeyed God, he became a blessing for all nations. When Jesus obeyed his Father, he redeemed the human race.

The "benefits" from a sociological standpoint are obvious. Stable parental structures produce well-adjusted children and therefore a better functioning society. Divine imperatives on marriage obligations act as a brake on the relentless promiscuity of males and the constant siren call of concupiscence. Procreation strictly within the framework of the family reinforces not just the parents' awareness of their obligations but also meets the emotional and physical needs of the children. Moreover, it is simply silly to suggest that the institutions of family or marriage are the products of evolutionary pressure: nothing in evolutionary theory calls for altruism, life-long devotion to one's young or love for one's parents. The chimpanzee mother who fiercely protects its child will mate with its child's killer. And parents are killed by their progeny not respected in the animal kingdom.

But the rules concerning the family are not to be followed simply because of their sociological benefits. Immeasurably more important is the fact that you can only "realize" your full potential, "grow" as a person, within this structure of true love. For to love is to give oneself to the other. Husband and wife one to the other, father and mother to the child, child to its parents. The family is a school of love. It is the earthly home that prepares for you for your heavenly home. (To be sure, children deprived of a stable family are not held responsible for any consequences that this might inflict on their development.) The obligations of each member of the family are laid out in the Bible along with the corresponding blessings. For instance, "Honor your father and your mother, that your days may be long in the land which the LORD your God gives you." (Exodus 20: 2-17).

The family is also a celebration of life. This is the structure within which God brings life into being, where life is a product of love and is, moreover, nurtured in love. Children are considered a blessing. When a woman has an abortion, she is not simply cooperating in the taking of innocent life, a violation of the Fifth Commandment ("You shall not kill"). She is in breach of her obligation as a mother by taking the life of her child instead of nourishing and protecting it.

There can be no home without a family and the Universe cannot be our home if we refuse to be part of the Family of its Creator. This is why the discovery of the Holy Family is timely and urgent.

We are called to live forever as members of a family, the Family of God. There is no remedy for the loneliness that crushes the soul other than the Love of the Father, the Son and the Holy Spirit, a love that is "hologrammed" in human terms by the Holy Family. And to enter this love is to enter Heaven.

Fundamental to the immediate and ultimate well-being of the family here and now is fidelity at several levels, fidelity to:

> the will of God
> one's spouse within a *permanent* union of *man and woman* [the mystery of "one flesh"] that is divinely constituted and *inter-penetrated*
> the fecundity gifted by God ("Go forth and multiply")
> the new life made possible by his direct intervention: "The man had intercourse with his wife Eve, and she conceived and gave birth to Cain, saying, "I have produced a male child with the help of the LORD." (Genesis: 4:1).
> the larger family of God (the Church)

Fidelity at all these levels is "built into" the very structure of human fulfillment and any breach weakens (and sometimes eviscerates) the lifeline to divinity and eternity and impoverishes earthly existence.

It is sobering indeed that Sr. Lucia, the surviving seer of Fatima, prophesied that the decisive battle between Jesus and Satan would be over marriage and family. In a letter to Cardinal Carlo Caffarra, the founding President of the John Paul II Institute of Marriage and Family, Sr. Lucia said:

> "Father, a time will come when the decisive battle between the kingdom of Christ and Satan will be over marriage and the family. And those who will work for the good of the family will experience persecution and tribulation. But do not be afraid, because Our Lady has already crushed his head."[23]

If we wish to know what Heaven has to say about the structure and mission of the family in modern times, we should turn to the pre-eminent apparition of the Holy Family: Fatima. Exegetes, theologians, philosophers, evolutionary biologists, psychologists, economists, anthropologists and sociologists have competing theories, perspectives and ideologies on the matter. But Fatima, an apparition known for dire warnings that came to pass and fulfilled prophecies, offers a unique insight into the divinely ordained blueprint for the family. So we will conclude this book with Sr. Lucia's account of this supernatural blueprint in her *Calls from the Message of Fatima*:

The Call to the Sanctification of the Family The Sixteenth Call of the Message.

God chose to conclude the Message in Fatima, in October 1917, with three further apparitions which I regard as three more calls placed before us for our consideration, so that we may keep them in mind during our earthly pilgrimage. While the people were gazing in astonishment at the sun which had gone pale in the light of the presence of God, the three children saw, beside the sun, three distinct and, to us, significant apparitions....

I propose to say quite simply what I think God wished to say to us with these apparitions.

The first was the apparition of the Holy Family: Our Lady, and the Child Jesus in the arms of St Joseph, blessing the people.

In times such as the present, when the family often seems misunderstood in the form in which it was established by God, and is assailed by doctrines that are erroneous and contrary to the purposes for which the Divine Creator instituted it, surely God wished to address to us a reminder of the purpose for which He established the family in the world?

God entrusted to the family the sacred mission of co-operating with Him in the work of creation. This decision to associate His poor creatures with His creative work is a great demonstration of the fatherly goodness of God. It is as if He were making them shares in His creative power; making use of His children in order to bring forth new lives, which will flower on earth but be destined for Heaven.

Thus the Divine Creator wished to entrust to the family a sacred mission, that makes two beings become one in union so close that it does not admit of separation. It is from this union that God wishes to produce other beings, as He generates flowers and fruit from the plants.

God established Matrimony as an indissoluble union. Once a couple have received the sacrament of Matrimony, the union between the two is definitive and cannot be broken; it is indissoluble as long as the couple remain alive. It was thus that God ordained it to be.

We read in the Book of Genesis: 'So God created man in his own image, in the image of God he created him; male and female he created them' (Gen 1, 27); two, yes, but these two are one: 'Therefore a man leaves his father and his mother and cleaves to his wife, and they become one flesh' (Gen 2, 24).

This is a law of God, which Jesus Christ confirmed and endorsed, in the face of human efforts, at that time, to pull in the opposite direction: "Have you not read that he who made them from the beginning made them male and female, and said "For this reason a man shall leave his father and mother and be joined to his wife, and the two shall become one. So they are no longer two but one. What therefore God has joined together, let no man put asunder"' (Mt 19, 4-6).

This is the law of Matrimony: from the time they had been joined together by the blessing of God, the two become one, and this union does not allow separation - What God has joined together, let no one put asunder. They become one by the bond of love that led them to commit themselves to each other in the ideal of co-operation with God in the work of creation, and this involves the sacrifice and immolation that the giving of oneself always implies; it involves, too, mutual understanding, forgiveness and pardon. It is thus that a home is built up, made holy and gives glory to God.

A home must be like a garden, where fresh rosebuds are opening, bringing to the world the freshness of innocence, a pure and trusting outlook on life, and the smile of innocent happy children. Only thus does God take pleasure in his creative work, blessing it and turning his fatherly gaze upon it. Any other way of behaving is to divert the work of God from its end, to alter the plans of God, failing to fulfill and carry out the mission that God has entrusted to the married couple.

Hence, in the Message of Fatima, God calls on us to turn our eyes to the Holy Family of Nazareth, into which He chose to be born, and to grow in grace and stature, in order to present to us a model to imitate, as our footsteps tread the path of our pilgrimage to Heaven.

The Evangelist St Luke, after describing for us how Jesus Christ, as a young boy, went up to the temple in Jerusalem where He got separated from His parents and there they found Him three days later, adds: 'And he went down with them and came to Nazareth, and was obedient to them; and his mother kept all these things in her heart.. And Jesus increased in wisdom and in stature, and in favour with God and man' (Lk 2, 51-52).

Parents who do not instill a knowledge of God and of His commandments into their children at an early age, teaching them to keep them in mind and to observe them, are failing to fulfill the mission entrusted to them by God. It is a law that God prescribed for His people: "And these words which I command you this day shall be upon your heart; and you shall teach them diligently to your children, and shall talk of them when you sit in your house, and when you walk by the way, and when you lie down, and when you rise" (Deut 6, 6-7). Parents who disregard this law of God make themselves responsible for the ignorance that is responsible for the disordered lives of the children who torment the declining years of their parents, and are themselves lost.

What has been said applies even when the children are entrusted to the care of competent teachers, because what remains most engraved in the hearts of children is what they have received in their father's arms and on their mother's lap. Nothing can dispense parents from this sublime mission: God has entrusted it to them and they are answerable to God for it.

Parents are the ones who must guide their children's first steps to the altar of God, teaching them to raise their innocent hands and to pray helping them to discover how to find God on their way and to follow the echo of his voice. This is the most serious and important mission that has been entrusted to God to parents; and they must fulfill it so well that throughout their lives, the memory of their parents will always arouse in their children the memory of God and of His teaching.

This is how St Paul encourages us to behave: "Children, obey your parents in the Lord, for this is right. 'Honour your father and mother' (this is the first commandment with a promise) "that it may be well with you and that you may live long on the earth" 'Fathers, do not provoke your children to anger but bring them up in the discipline and instruction of the Lord'" (Eph 6, 1-4). And in the second letter of St John, which was undoubtedly addressed to an ecclesial community, but which he sees personified in the person of a mother - the elect lady and her children- we find from the pen of the Apostle, a eulogy that we wish could be applied to all fathers and mothers: "I rejoice greatly to find some of your children following the truth, just as we have been commanded by the Father. And now I beg you, lady, not as though I were writing you a new commandment, but the one we have had from the beginning, that we love one another" (2Jn 4-5).

In families composed of parents and children, there are duties which the parents have to fulfill in relation to their children, and vice versa, the children in relation to their parents. The Book of Sirach (Ecclesiasticus), after listing the many duties of children, concludes with this appeal to their submission and gentleness: "My son, perform your tasks in meekness; then you will be loved by those who God accepts. The greater you are, the more you must humble yourself; so you will find favour in the sight of the Lord. For great is the might of the Lord; he is glorified by the humble" (Sir 3, 17-20). And the Apostle St Peter presses home the same idea: "Likewise you that are younger be subject to the elders. Clothe yourselves, all of you, with humility towards one another, for God opposes the proud, but gives grace to the humble. Humble yourselves therefore under the mighty hand of God, that in due time he may exalt you. Cast all your anxieties on him, for he cares about you. Be sober, be watchful." (1 Pet 5, 5-8).

These words are addressed to us all, but especially to the young people who have as yet no experience of life, which is why the Apostle urges them to be submissive, sober and vigilant, in order not to be taken in by the illusions of life, by the disordered appetites of nature, and the diabolical seductions of the world. Because - St Peter goes on - "Your adversary the devil prowls around like a roaring lion, seeking some one to devour. Resist him, firm in your faith, knowing that the same experience of suffering is required of your brotherhood throughout the world. And after you have suffered a little while, the God of all grace, who has called you to his eternal glory in Christ, will himself restore, establish, and strengthen you. (1 Pet 5, 8-10). Yes firm in faith, in hope and in charity, we must all struggle to achieve victory over evil, and attain the peace, joy and blessedness of the house of Our Father who is God; and we altogether form his family.

The children must never forget or set to one side the respect, gratitude and help which they owe to their parents, who are for them the image of God. In fact, just as the parents sacrificed themselves in order to bring the children up, educate and establish their children in life, so the children, in turn have a duty to sacrifice themselves in order to give pleasure, joy and serenity to their parents, aiding and assisting them, if necessary, in such away that everything is done out of true love and with one's eyes fixed on God: "Whatever your task, work heartily, as serving the Lord and not men, knowing that from the Lord you will receive the inheritance as your reward; you are serving the Lord Christ." (Col 3, 23). And we shall enjoy his friendship, as He has told us: "You are my friends if you do what I command you" (Jn 15, 14) And what has He commanded us? "This is my commandment, that you love one another as I have loved you" (Jn 15, 12).

This is how a family sanctifies itself, grows and prospers in that unity, fidelity, mutual understanding and forgiveness which generate peace, joy, mutual trust and love. Ave Maria!

Notes

[1] "The Holy Family: The Emergence of Devotion in the Church by Aine Hayd https://www.holyfamilybordeaux.org/wp-content/uploads/2015/08/Emergence-of-devotion-to-The-Holy-Family1.pdf

[2] http://www.holyfamilybordeaux.org/wp-content/media/2012/09/Emergence-of-devotion-to-The-Holy-Family1.pdf

[3] Joseph F. Chorpenning, The Holy Family Devotion – A Brief History (Montreal, Canada: Centre de Recherche et de documentation, 1997), 6.

[4] Ibid, 7-8.

[5] Ibid, 16-17.

[6] Ibid, 20.

[7] Ibid, 27-9.

[8] Ibid, 32-3, 6.

[9] *The Spiritual Conferences of St. Francis de Sales*, translated by F. Aidan Gasquet, O.S.B. and Henry Benedict Mackey, O.S.B. (1906; Westminster, Maryland: Newman Press: 1962), 374.

[10] Aine Hayde, "The Holy Family: The Emergence of Devotion in the Church," http://www.holyfamilybordeaux.org/wp-content/media/2012/09/Emergence-of-devotion-to-The-Holy-Family1.pdf.

[11] Ibid.

[12] Chorpenning, op cit., 43-4.

[13] Ibid., 51.

[14] Ibid., 53.

[15] Ibid., 55.

[16] Dominic de Domenico, *True Devotion to St. Joseph and the Church* (Kentucky: New Hope Publications, 2003).

[17] J. Ferrer Arellano, "The Virginal Marriage of Mary and Joseph according to Bl. John Duns Scotus", in Bl. John Duns Scotus and His Mariology, Commemoration of the Seventh Centenary of His Death, Acts of the Symposium on Scotus' Mariology, Grey College, Durham - England (New Bedford, 2009).

[18]"The Customary of Our Lady of Walsingham," http://latinhymns.blogspot.com/2020/12/

[19]John Paul II, *Puebla: A Pilgrimage of Faith* (Boston: Daughters of Saint Paul, 1979), 86.

[20]*Letter to Families*, 6.

[21]*Christifideles Laici*, 52

[22]Marc Ouellet, *Divine Likeness: Toward a Trinitarian Anthropology of the Family* (Grand Rapids, MI: Wm. B. Eerdmans, 2006)

[23]https://aleteia.org/2017/05/19/exclusive-cardinal-caffarra-what-sr-lucia-wrote-to-me-is-being-fulfilled-today/